Nelson MATHEMATICS 5

towards LEVEL 5 and Beyond

PUPILS'

BOOK 2

Nelson

Thomas Nelson and Sons Ltd
Nelson House Mayfield Road
Walton-on-Thames Surrey
KT12 5PL UK

51 York Place
Edinburgh
EH1 3JD UK

Thomas Nelson (Hong Kong) Ltd
Toppan Building 10/F
22A Westlands Road
Quarry Bay Hong Kong

Thomas Nelson Australia
102 Dodds Street
South Melbourne
Victoria 3205
Australia

Nelson Canada
1120 Birchmount Road
Scarborough Ontario
M1K 5G4 Canada

Authors and consultants
Bill Domoney
Peter Gash
Paul Harrison
Lorely James
David Kirkby
Ann Sawyer
Diana Wright

Contributors
Paul Broadbent
Brenda Stevens

Acknowledgements

Photography
Biofotos: pages 55, 100; Colorsport: pages 36, 66
(bottom); Greg Evans: page 58; Chris Ridgers: pages 32,
66 (top); Zefa: page 93.

Design
Julia King, Thumbnail Graphics

Illustration
Phillip Burrows
Jane Cheswright
Karen Donnelly
Jackie East
Stan Stevens
Kareen Taylerson
Charles Whelon

Produced by **AMR**

First published by Thomas Nelson & Sons Ltd 1993

ISBN 0-17-421634-3 (single copies)
ISBN 0-17-421635-1 (pack of 6)
NPN 9 8 7 6 5 4 3 2 1

Printed in Hong Kong

CONTENTS

The colour band at the foot of each page indicates the relevant section of the **Teacher's Resource File, Level 5 and Beyond.**

Number

Whole number
Alternative methods of multiplying **4–5**
Dividing by multiples of 10 **6–7**
Dividing remainders **44–45**
Mayan and Babylonian numbers **46–47**
Mental calculation **84–85**
Base 10 and binary **86–87**

Factors, multiples and powers
Investigating lowest common multiples **8–9**
Square and cube numbers **48–49**
Powers of 10 **88**
Prime factors **89**

Positive and negative numbers
Ordered pairs with negative numbers **10–11**
Base and index **50–51**
Patterns and magic squares **90–91**

Decimal number
Multiplying decimals **12–15**
Missing decimals and points **52–53**
Decimal points and place value **54–55**
Mental division, measurement and money **92–93**
Remainders and value for money **94–95**
Currency rates **96–97**

Fractions, decimals and percentages
Equivalent fractions **16–17**
Converting between fractions, percentages and
decimals **56–57**
Calculating percentages and discounts **98–99**

Ratio
Scale drawing **18–19**
The golden ratio and rectangles **58–59**
The golden spiral **100**
Golden ratio in numbers **101**

Algebra

Patterns
Investigating the golden ratio **20**
Number patterns and calculators **21**
Equivalent fractions and recurring decimals **60–63**
Using spreadsheets **102–103**

Functions
Graphs of functions **22–23, 64–65**
Functions in spreadsheets **104–105**

Measures

Making, recording and using measures
Significant figures and accuracy **24–25**
Speed, distance and time **26–27, 66**
Reading scales **67**
Greater heights **106**
Volumes of prisms **107**

Shape and Space

Exploring properties of shapes
Parallelograms **28–29**
Trapeziums **30–31**
Kites **68, 70–71**
Arrowheads **69, 71**
Classifying quadrilaterals **108–109**

Location and transformation of shapes
Plans of 3-D objects **32–33, 72–73**
Reflection **34–35**
Rotation **74–75**
Centres of rotation **110–111**
Similarity and congruency **112**
Enlargement **113**

Angles
Angles and parallel lines **36–37**
Classifying triangles **76**
Finding unknown angles **77, 114–115**
Interior and exterior angles of polygons **116–117**
Constructing angles and shapes with compass and
ruler **118–119**

Handling Data

Collecting, processing and interpreting data
Mean, median, mode and range **38–39, 78–79**

Representing and interpreting data
Scatter diagrams **40–41, 80–81**
Choosing ways to represent data **120–121**

Handling data contexts
Analysing diet and ingredients **122–123**

Probability
Assigning a numerical value **42–43**
Weather prediction **82**
Games and chance **83**
Comparing probability with outcomes **124–125**

Glossary 126–128

Multiplying with boxes

Different countries have developed different ways of working with numbers.

The Gelosia method might have been used in India to work out the multiplication 234 x 36. Try it for yourself:

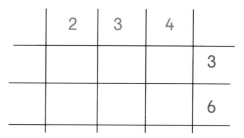

1. First draw a grid and print the numbers to be multiplied along the top and down the side.

   Draw diagonals through the grid.

   Multiply pairs of digits and put the answers in the correct box.
   (If it is a single-digit answer, put a zero (0) in front of it.)

   Add the single digits in each diagonal.
   If the answer has 2 digits then carry it forward.
   For example,
   8 + 2 + 2 = 12.

   The answer is read from top left to bottom right: 8424

   Try and see why it works.

Use the Gelosia method to try these:

2. 291 x 13   3. 164 x 27

4. 339 x 42   5. 462 x 33

6. Try the Gelosia method for numbers with more digits.

Choose your method

Here are some other multiplications. Try and solve them without a calculator. Choose your own method.

1. 42 x 239
2. 332 x 79
3. 155 x 98
4. 469 x 61
5. 497 x 43
6. 199 x 49

7. Shackleton's electric shop takes delivery of 24 colour televisions. Each one costs £114.
   How much will they cost altogether?

8. The shop also took delivery of 15 camcorders at £799 each. What was the total cost of these?

9. The manager bought 125 electric plugs to fit to items in the shop. Each plug cost 63p. What was the total cost?

10. To complete the delivery, there were 25 extension cables at £8.99 each. What was the total cost of these?

Mental division

Try these in your head.
Check them with a calculator.

1. 670 ÷ 10
2. 67 ÷ 10
3. 1900 ÷ 100
4. 190 ÷ 100
5. 4000 ÷ 1000
6. 400 ÷ 1000
7. What happens to the digits of any number divided by 10, by 100, by 1000?

Now try these:

8. 140 ÷ 20
9. 480 ÷ 60
10. 180 ÷ 30
11. 720 ÷ 90
12. Write instructions for dividing any number by 30.

Division problems

Choose your own method to solve these problems.
Do them in your head if you can.

1. 500 metres of cable are cut into 20 metre lengths.
   How many lengths are there?

2. £12.60 was left over after a school trip.
   It was shared equally between a class of 30 children.
   How much did each child get?

3. Many books are printed in sections of 32 pages.
   How many sections are put together to make a book
   of 448 pages?

4. The books are packed into boxes of 24.
   How many boxes are needed for 264 books?

5. Jo needs £4.50 to buy a new book.
   If she saves £0.25 per week, how long will it take her
   to get the book?

There is more about division on page 44.

Looking at multiples

Clare changes her oil every 3 weeks. She changes her spark plugs every 5 weeks.

To find out how often she does both jobs together you can use multiples.

First, list the multiples of 3 and 5.

Multiples of 3: 3, 6, 9, 12, 15, 18, 21, 24, 27, 30 ...

Multiples of 5: 5, 10, 15, 20, 25, 30, 35 ...

Notice that 15 and 30 are multiples of both 3 and 5.

Multiples common to 2 numbers are called common multiples

So 15 and 30 are common multiples of 3 and 5.

15 is the lowest common multiple of 3 and 5.

1. List the first 10 multiples of 4 and 6.

2. Which multiples are common?

3. Which is the lowest common multiple?

Find the lowest common multiple of these pairs of numbers:

4. 6, 8

5. 3, 14

6. 9, 15

7. 4, 5

8. 5, 7

9. 3, 9

Testing before dividing

Before you divide a number, you can check to see if it will divide exactly.

If the final digit is 0, 2, 4, 6 or 8, the number will divide by 2. For example, 12, 26.

If the sum of the digits is a multiple of 3, the number will divide by 3. For example, 12, 18.

If the last two digits are a multiple of 4, the number will divide by 4. For example, 24, 116.

If the final digits are 5 or 0, it will divide by 5. For example, 25, 40.

If the sum of the digits is a multiple of 9, the number will divide by 9. For example, 18, 72.

If the final digit is 0, it will divide by 10. For example, 20, 120.

Test these numbers.
For each number say whether it will divide by 2, 3, 4, 5, 9 and 10.

1. 522   2. 720   3. 1806   4. 4455   5. 2100

6. 1001   7. 736   8. 8613   9. 1136   10. 1762

11. 729   12. 111   13. 9724   14. 6561   15. 771

There is more about dividing exactly on page 92.

Positive and negative ordered pairs

These x and y axes have positive and negative numbers.

Remember: in an ordered pair, the number on the x-axis comes first.

This rectangle is drawn by joining 4 points. One of the points is (−5, −2). It is marked for you.

Write the ordered pairs for the other 3 points.

1.   2.   3.

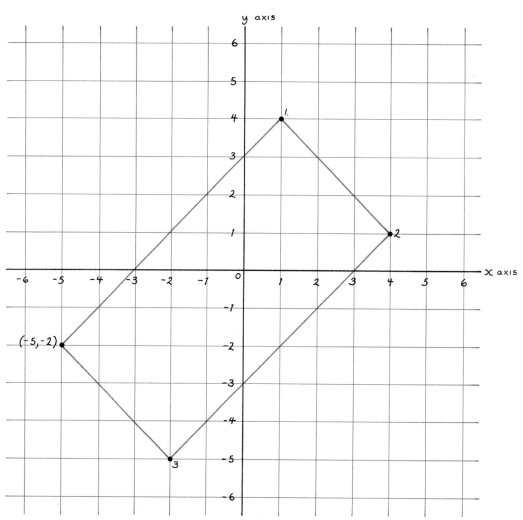

Draw them yourself

These show half of two symmetrical shapes.

Copy the axes and the half-shapes. Draw the other half of the shapes and write down the co-ordinates of the vertices.

1.

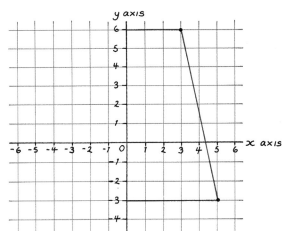

2.

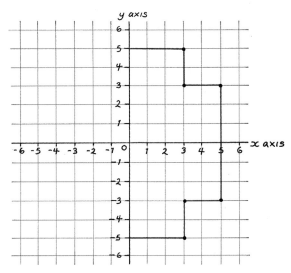

Draw your own axes. Plot the co-ordinates.

Join them up and name the shape.

3. (2, 6) (6, −3) (−2, −3)

4. (−3, 3) (3, 3) (3, −3) (−3, −3)

5. (−3, 2) (5, 2) (2, −2) (−6, −2)

6. (−1, 5) (2, 2) (−1, −6) (−3, 2)

7. Draw your own shape on positive and negative axes. Give the co-ordinates to a friend and ask him or her to draw it.

There is more about positive and negative numbers on page 90.

Multiplying decimals

Before you multiply decimal numbers it is helpful to estimate the answer first:

1.75 x 2

1.75 is nearly 2, and 2 x 2 is 4 so the answer should be less than 4. (It is 3.5)

Estimate the answer to these first, then calculate.

Compare your estimate with the answer.

1. 1.85 x 3

2. 5.1 x 5

3. 12.3 x 4

4. 6.9 x 2

5. 9.95 x 6

6. 14.5 x 3

7. 7.75 x 4

8. 2.25 x 8

Estimate and then check the answers to these:

9. Mrs. Downes collected £2.50 from each of 8 children. How much did she collect altogether?

10. 6 children each made a Christmas decoration 1.5 m long. When they were joined together, how long was the whole decoration?

Multiplying decimals by big numbers

1. Complete this chart.

Decimal Number	x 10	x 20	x 30	x 50	x 100
1.6	16	32	48		
3.5	35	70			
7.8	78				
12.9					
15.25					
18.75					
25.55					
50.05					

2. Describe how the numbers change when you multiply by 10 and by 100.

The answers to these multiplications have the decimal points missing. Write them out correctly.

3. 4.2 x 4 = 168

4. 3.25 x 5 = 1625

5. 12.95 x 3 = 3885

6. 20.01 x 8 = 16008

7. 5.15 x 7 = 3605

8. 15.375 x 4 = 615

There is more about decimals on page 52.

Changing decimal numbers

Copy and complete this chart.
Put in 5 more decimal numbers of your own.

	Decimal Number	x 100	x 10	x 1	x 0.1	x 0.01
1.	4.3	430	43	4.3	0.43	0.043
2.	2.71					
3.	12.5					
4.	22.25					
5.	1.375					
6.	15.143					

Look carefully at the numbers in the chart.

7. Describe how the digits move in relation to the decimal point.

Estimate the answers

Remember: an approximate answer will tell you where the decimal point goes.

Estimate which answer is correct. (You can check afterwards.)

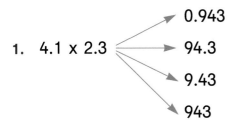

1. 4.1 x 2.3
- 0.943
- 94.3
- 9.43
- 943

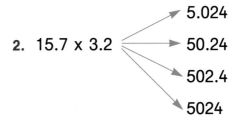

2. 15.7 x 3.2
- 5.024
- 50.24
- 502.4
- 5024

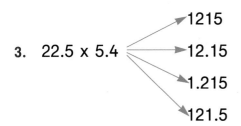

3. 22.5 x 5.4
- 1215
- 12.15
- 1.215
- 121.5

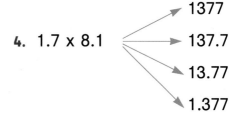

4. 1.7 x 8.1
- 1377
- 137.7
- 13.77
- 1.377

Estimate the answers to these first.

Then use mental arithmetic, pencil and paper or a calculator to check your estimate against the true answers.

5. 4.6 x 1.8　　　　　　6. 3.1 x 2.6

7. 12.5 x 3.5　　　　　　8. 4.2 x 3.3

9. 8.4 x 9.9　　　　　10. 19.8 x 2.1

There is more about decimals on page 54.

Equivalent fractions

Remember: equivalent fractions have the same value.

1. Copy and complete this chart of equivalent fractions.

fraction	quarters	fifths	sixths	eighths	tenths
$\frac{1}{2}$	$\frac{2}{4}$	—	$\frac{3}{6}$	$\frac{4}{8}$	$\frac{5}{10}$
$\frac{1}{3}$	—	—	$\frac{2}{6}$	—	—
$\frac{2}{3}$					
$\frac{1}{4}$					
$\frac{3}{4}$					
$\frac{1}{5}$					
$\frac{2}{5}$					
$\frac{3}{5}$					
$\frac{4}{5}$					

In a family of equivalent fractions the simplest fraction is the one with the lowest numerator and denominator.

Use the chart to find the simplest equivalent fraction for each of these:

2. $\frac{5}{10}$ 3. $\frac{6}{8}$ 4. $\frac{4}{6}$ 5. $\frac{6}{10}$

6. Make another chart to show twelfths, twentieths and hundredths.

Fraction problems

You can use equivalent fractions or towers of cubes
to help with problems like $2\frac{2}{3} - 1\frac{1}{4}$.

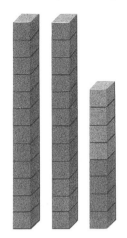

$2\frac{2}{3}$ is
2 towers of 12
and 8 cubes.

$\frac{32}{12}$

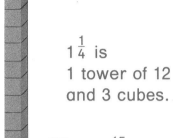

$1\frac{1}{4}$ is
1 tower of 12
and 3 cubes.

$\frac{15}{12}$

$\frac{32}{12} - \frac{15}{12} = \frac{17}{12}$

$\frac{17}{12}$ is top heavy, so we change it to $1\frac{5}{12}$

Use towers of 12 cubes to solve these:

1. $1\frac{1}{2} + 1\frac{1}{4}$

2. $2\frac{1}{4} - 1\frac{1}{6}$

3. $2\frac{2}{3} + 2\frac{1}{4}$

4. $1\frac{2}{3} + 2\frac{1}{2}$

5. $1\frac{3}{4} - 1\frac{2}{3}$

Use towers of 10 cubes to solve these:

6. $2\frac{3}{5} - 1\frac{3}{10}$

7. $2\frac{1}{2} + 2\frac{1}{10}$

8. $2\frac{1}{2} - 1\frac{1}{5}$

Choose towers to solve these:

9. $2\frac{3}{8} - 2\frac{1}{4}$

10. $2\frac{1}{4} - 1\frac{1}{5}$

Scaling up

A ratio can describe how much to enlarge a drawing. A ratio of 3:1 means 3 cm on the new drawing for every 1 cm on the old.

Enlarge these shapes in the ratio shown. You may need to use A4 sheets of paper.

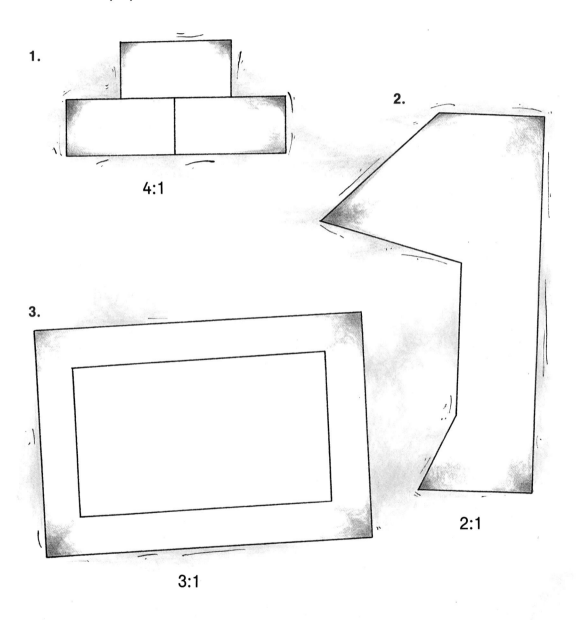

1.

4:1

2.

2:1

3.

3:1

Scaling down

A ratio can also describe how to shrink (reduce) a drawing. A ratio of 1:3 means 1 cm on the new drawing for every 3 cm on the old.

Reduce this pattern of wooden beams in the ratio 1:3.

There is more about scale on page 106.

Whirling squares

1. Draw a rectangle 2 x 1, made up of 2 squares (a domino).
   Draw a square on the longer side. Repeat the process.

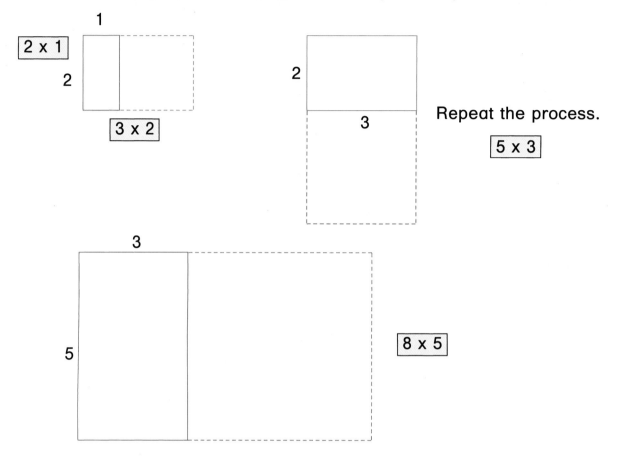

Repeat the process.

2. Carry on drawing the rectangles.

3. Describe how the sequence is growing.

4. Predict the dimensions of the 10th rectangle.

This pattern is related to the golden ratio.

There is more about the golden ratio on page 58.

Patterns   Unit 2   Investigating the dimensions of a series of rectangles

Calculator patterns

A calculator can be used to help discover patterns.

For example, there is a pattern in these multiplication statements:

37 x 3
37 x 33
37 x 333
37 x 3333
37 x 33333

1. Is there a pattern in the products?

2. Describe your results.

Use a calculator to find the products of these
multiplication statements.
Can you predict the next 3 in each series?
Describe the patterns.

3. 9 x 6   4. 91 x 44   5.   1 x 9
    9 x 66   91 x 444   12 x 9
    9 x 666   91 x 4444   123 x 9
    9 x 6666   91 x 44444   1234 x 9

6. Now try this: 143 x 1 x 7
                143 x 2 x 7
                143 x 3 x 7

7. Can you predict the result for 143 x 9 x 7?

8. Try 143 x 100 x 7, 143 x 101 x 7, and so on.

There is more about patterns on page 62.

Drawing graphs of functions

You will need graph paper.

You can show a function, like x 3 + 1, as a graph. First make a chart showing several results.

number	function x 3 + 1
x axis	y axis
1	4
2	7
3	10
4	13

Then plot the points on graph paper as ordered pairs: (1,4) (2,7) (3,10) (4,13)

Join the points with a line.

You can extend the line as far as you like, above and below 0.

Draw a graph for each of these functions. Beside each one, write the value on the y axis if the x axis is –2, 8, and 10.

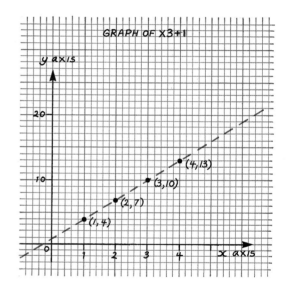

1. x 4 + 3   2. x 3 –6   3. –4 x 2

Find the function

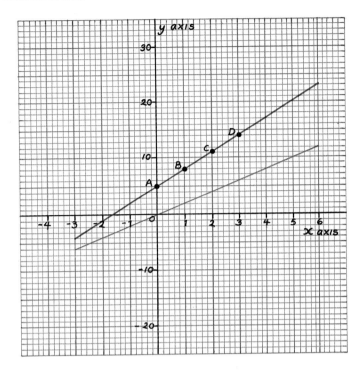

At point A the value of x is 0.
The value of y is 5.

So A is the point (0, 5).

What are the x and y values (x,y) for:

1. B?   2. C?   3. D?

Complete the chart by filling in the y values.

x axis	y axis
0	5
1	
2	
3	
4	

4. What is the hidden function machine
    connecting x and y?

5. On the blue line what are the values for y
    when x = 0, 1, 2, 3 and 4?
    What is the hidden function machine
    connecting x and y?

 There is more about graphs and functions on page 65.

Reading scales

When we write down measurements, the significant figures are those we have actually been able to measure. For example, 29.1 cm if we had measured to the nearest tenth of a centimetre. If we then convert from one unit of measure to another, the number of significant figures stays the same.

For example, 29.1 cm = 291 mm = 0.291 m
Each of these is accurate to 3 significant figures.

Here is part of a metre ruler.

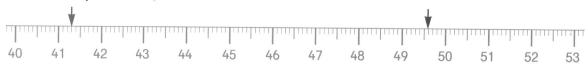

The blue arrow is closest to the 41.3 cm mark. It shows 41.3 cm to 3 significant figures.

1. Between which 2 marks does the red arrow lie?

2. Which mark is it closest to?

Write the length in:

3. cm accurate to 3 significant figures.

4. m accurate to 3 significant figures.

5. mm accurate to 3 significant figures.

6. Which 2 points on the scale does the fluid lie between?

7. Which point is it closest to?

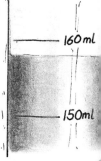

Write the capacity:

8. in ml accurate to 2 significant figures?

9. litres accurate to 2 significant figures.

10. Estimate the capacity in ml accurate to 3 significant figures.

There is more about measuring with significant figures on page 67.

Making, recording and using measures   Unit 4   Reading scales and recording with significant figures

Measuring within limits

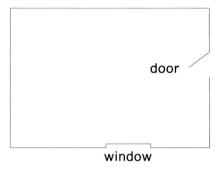

Ruth measured her living room as accurately as she could with a tape measure. The length was between 5.3 m and 5.4 m.
The breadth was between 3.6 m and 3.7 m.

1. What is the greatest the area could be?

2. What is the least the area could be?

3. What is the difference between the greatest and least area?

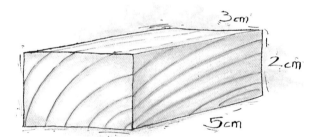

This wooden brick was made as accurately as possible. Each dimension could still be 1 mm more or less than stated.

4. What is the least volume it could have?

5. What is the greatest volume it could have?

6. What is the difference between the least and greatest volumes?

Measure a table in your classroom carefully. Calculate its area, show a minimum and maximum possible area.

Moving quickly

Simon timed Layla as she ran between 2 points 25 m apart.

1st run	5½ secs
2nd run	5 secs
3rd run	4½ secs
4th run	5 secs

1. What was Layla's average time for 25 m?

2. At this speed how long would it take to run 100 m?

3. How fast is she running in metres per second?

4. A mile is approximately 1609 m. How many minutes and seconds would it take Layla to run a mile?

5. What is her approximate speed in miles per hour?

Get a friend to time you over 25 m. Work out how fast you ran in miles per hour.

There is more about running speed on page 66.

Making, recording and using measures   Unit 5   *Converting speeds*

Graphing journeys

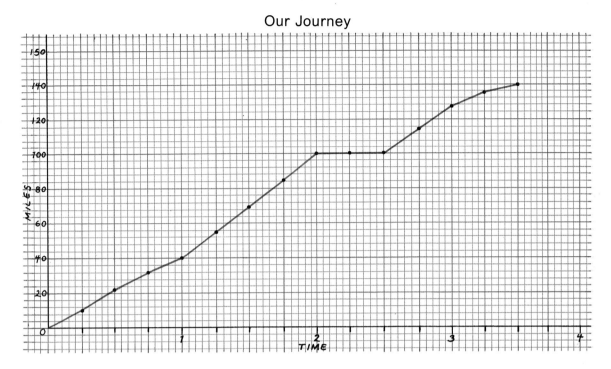

Our Journey

MILES / TIME

Ruth and Bill used the milometer on the car and their watches to draw a graph of their car journey from Oxford to Sheffield. Every 15 minutes they recorded how far they had travelled.

What was their average speed for:

1. the first hour?

2. the second hour?

3. the whole journey?

4. Write the story of the journey. Explain the changes in speed.

Constructing parallelograms

You will need a ruler, pencil and protractor.

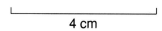
4 cm

1. To construct a parallelogram with sides of 4 cm and 3 cm and with angles of 70° and 110°, first draw a baseline 4 cm long.

Use a protractor to mark an angle of 70° at one end and 110° at the other end.

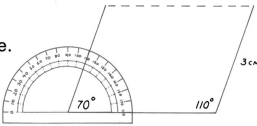

Draw the 3 cm sides.
Finally draw the missing side.

Draw these parallelograms. You will need to measure them very carefully first.

2.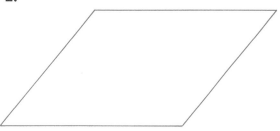

3.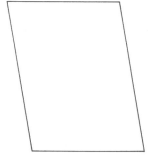

Now draw parallelograms with these measurements.

4. Sides 5 cm and 7 cm.
   Angles 60° and 120°.

5. Sides 3 cm and 6 cm.
   Angles 40° and 140°.

6. Sides 8 cm and 10 cm.
   Angles 45° and 135°.

7. Sides 9 cm and 12 cm.
   Angles 75° and 105°.

Special parallelograms

Remember: a parallelogram has 2 pairs of parallel sides.

Here are some special parallelograms.

A rectangle is a parallelogram with right angles.

A rhombus is a parallelogram with 4 equal sides.

A square is a parallelogram with 4 equal sides and right angles. A square is a special rhombus.

Use a ruler and protractor and / or a computer drawing program to draw:

1. a square and another rhombus with side lengths of 5 cm.

2. a rectangle and another parallelogram with side lengths of 3 cm and 5 cm.

3. a rhombus with side lengths of 4 cm and internal angles of 50° and 130°.

4. a parallelogram with side lengths of 6 cm and 3 cm and internal angles of 60° and 120°.

Trapeziums from squares

A trapezium is a quadrilateral with one pair of parallel sides.

 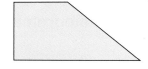 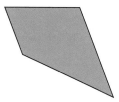

Divide a square into 2 pieces like this:

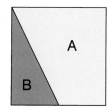

1. Cut and rearrange A and B to make a trapezium.
   You can turn pieces over if you want to.
   Sketch the trapezium you make.

Divide a square into 3 pieces like this:

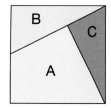

2. Make a trapezium using A and B. Sketch it.

3. Make a trapezium using A and C. Sketch it.

4. Make a trapezium using B and C. Sketch it.

5. Make a trapezium using A, B and C. Sketch it.

Trapeziums and gates

Here are some trapeziums.

a.

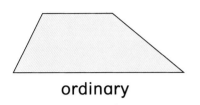

ordinary

b.

right-angled

c.

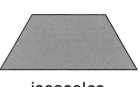

isosceles

1. Which of them have one or more lines of symmetry?

2. Which of them tessellate?

Sketch this five-bar gate.

3. How many isosceles trapeziums are there?

4. Colour 3 different right-angled trapeziums.

Look out for other five-bar gates. See what shapes you can find.

Drawing three-dimensional objects

It is difficult to draw a three-dimensional object.

Designers use different views to overcome this problem.

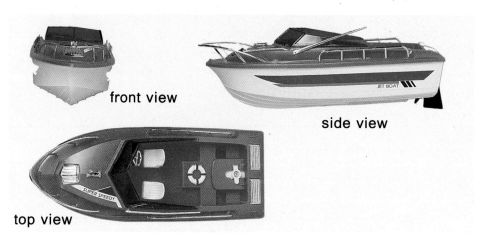

front view

side view

top view

Name these objects from the views shown.

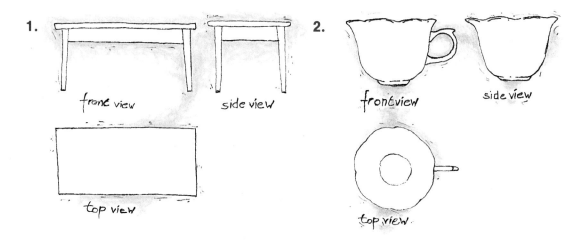

1. front view   side view

   top view

2. front view   side view

   top view

3. Make 3 drawings of an object in your classroom showing front, side and top views.

More plans and views

Identify these household objects from the view shown.

1.

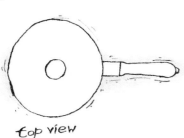

top view

2.

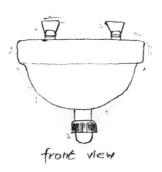

front view

3.

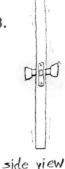

side view

Name these solid shapes from the views shown.

4.

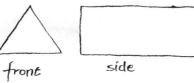

front   side

5.

front   side

6.

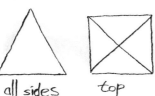

all sides   top

7.

front   top

8. Use cubes to make this model. Draw its top view, side view and front view.

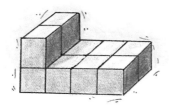

9. Make your own model from cubes and draw all 3 views.

There is more about drawing three-dimensional objects on page 72.

Reflecting shapes

You can transform shapes drawn
on paper by reflecting them in a
mirror.

This blue triangle has been
transformed into a kite.

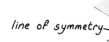

The line where the mirror joins
the shape is the line of symmetry.

Trace each of these shapes.

Put a mirror along the red line and draw the reflection.

1. 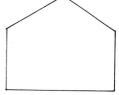   2. 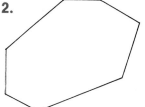   3.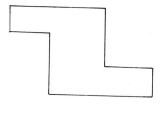

Copy these pairs of shapes on to squared paper. Draw a red line to
show where the mirror was placed to draw the reflection.

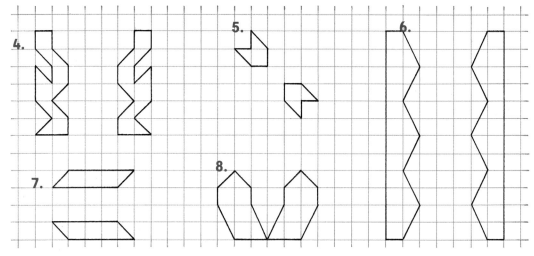

Reflected shapes

The green shape is a reflection in the y axis of the red shape.

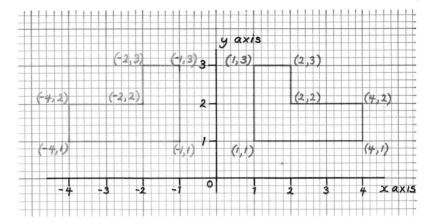

Copy these shapes on to graph paper. Draw their reflections in the y axis. Write the co-ordinates for each shape.

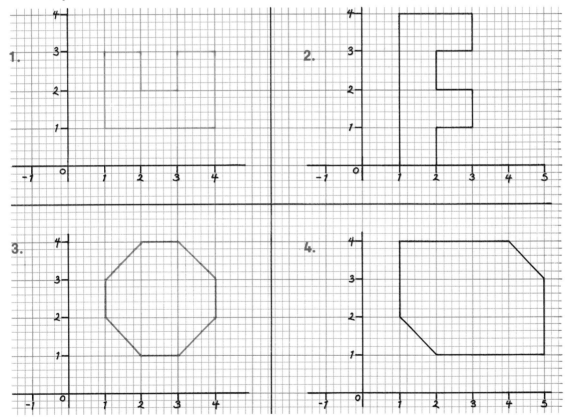

1.

2.

3.

4.

5. Draw your own shapes and reflections on graph paper. Write the co-ordinates.

Parallel lines and their angles

When a line intersects (cuts across) two parallel lines, 8 angles are formed.

There are 4 angles inside (interior angles) and 4 angles outside (exterior angles)

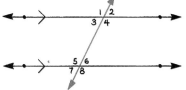

They can be looked at as pairs like this:

The alternate interior angles are equal and form a Z pattern.

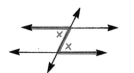

These angles are called corresponding angles. They are equal and form an F pattern.

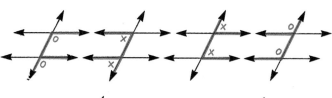

These are called co-interior angles. They add up to 180° and form a ⌐ pattern.

1. Trace this diagram and extend the lines. Measure each angle, then copy and complete the table.

Angle	1	2	3	4	5	6	7	8
Measure								

2. List the pairs of alternate interior angles and their measures.

3. List the pairs of corresponding angles and their measures.

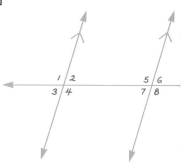

4. List the pairs of co-interior angles and their measures.

Parallel lines in real life

Lines intersecting parallel lines are found in real life.

1. Draw this five-barred gate accurately.

Colour in one pair of each of these:

2. alternate interior angles (red)

3. corresponding angles (blue)

4. co-interior angles (green)

5. Write the sizes of the angles formed by the line intersecting the parallel lines.

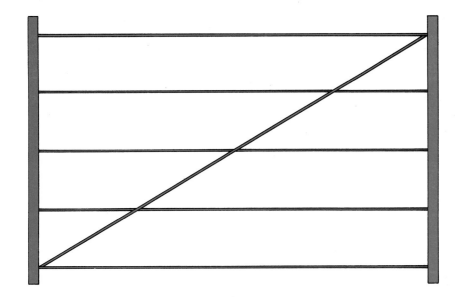

6. Look for other examples of lines intersecting parallel lines in real life.

Sorting out scores

> Remember: mean, mode and median are all different types of average.

Mr. O'Reilly gave the class back their maths tests.

He arranged the scores in order.

100
95
90
85
80 ➡ The score in the middle (80) is the median.
75
75
70
65

The score that occurred most often (75) is the mode.

He calculated the mean score by adding all the scores and dividing by the number of scores:
100 + 95 + 90 + 80 + 75 + 75 + 70 + 65 = 735

735 ÷ 9 = 81.67

He calculated the range by subtracting the lowest score from the highest score: 100 − 65 = 35

Here are the scores for the class English test:
38, 60, 25, 71, 42, 52, 50, 43, 65, 50, 76, 34, 50

1. Arrange the scores in order.
2. What is the median score?
3. Which score is the mode?
4. Calculate the mean score.
5. What is the range of scores?

Homework times

Linda surveyed some children in her class about the number of minutes they spent on homework the previous evening.
They gave her their times on slips of paper.

1. Order the times.

2. What was the mean amount of time spent?

3. Whose time was nearest to the mean?

4. What was the median time?

5. Which children spent the median amount of time?

6. What was the mode amount of time spent?

7. What was the range of times?

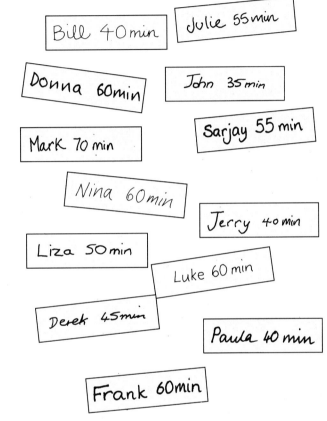

Bill 40 min

Julie 55 min

Donna 60 min

John 35 min

Mark 70 min

Sarjay 55 min

Nina 60 min

Jerry 40 min

Liza 50 min

Luke 60 min

Derek 45 min

Paula 40 min

Frank 60 min

8. Carry out your own survey.

Does your class do homework? Or you could find out how many minutes children spend on maths in a day or a week.

Find the range, median, mode and mean of your data.

There is more about mean, median, mode and range on page 78.

Body measures

Name	Hand Length	Foot Length	Ankle Circumference	Waist
Khuran	19 cm	28.5 cm	24.5 cm	81 cm
Laura	15 cm	19 cm	17 cm	95 cm
Kelly	17.5 cm	22.5 cm	16 cm	56 cm
Nick	18 cm	22.5 cm	18 cm	83 cm
Russell	15.5 cm	22 cm	16.5 cm	62 cm
Anita	14 cm	18 cm	16.5 cm	57 cm
Melanie	18 cm	25 cm	24 cm	70.5 cm
Ian	10 cm	13 cm	13.5 cm	56 cm
Emma	14 cm	16 cm	17 cm	65 cm
Umeed	19.5 cm	29 cm	24 cm	75 cm
Hitesh	21.5 cm	28 cm	21 cm	60 cm
Jenny	20 cm	26 cm	21.5 cm	96 cm
Kathleen	22 cm	31 cm	22 cm	85 cm
Martin	19.5 cm	27 cm	21 cm	88 cm
Simon	19 cm	25.5 cm	20.5 cm	50 cm
Ricki	19.5 cm	26 cm	22 cm	50.5 cm
Kerry	20 cm	27.5 cm	24 cm	88 cm
Yasmin	22.5 cm	31.5 cm	29 cm	84.5 cm
Tony	20.5 cm	26.5 cm	24 cm	96 cm
Anita	22 cm	28.5 cm	25 cm	60.5 cm
Fawad	20 cm	29.5 cm	25.5 cm	75 cm
Amy	14.5 cm	16.5 cm	16.5 cm	64.5 cm
Robyn	10.5 cm	13.5 cm	14 cm	56 cm
Angela	18.5 cm	25.5 cm	21 cm	71 cm
Simran	14.5 cm	18.5 cm	16 cm	57 cm
Tom	16 cm	22.5 cm	20.5 cm	61.5 cm
Paul	18.5 cm	23 cm	16.5 cm	83 cm
Vijay	18 cm	23 cm	18 cm	56.5 cm
Balbir	15.5 cm	19.5 cm	21 cm	95 cm
Jamie	19.5 cm	29 cm	24.5 cm	80.5 cm

Use this database to answer the questions on the next page.

Is there a correlation?

Look at the database on page 40.

Do you think that there is a relationship between foot length and hand length?

Do children with the longer feet tend to have the longer hands?

Do children with the shorter feet tend to have the shorter hands?

If there is, we say there is a correlation between foot length and hand length.

To see if there is a correlation, you will need to make a scatter diagram.

Here is how you make it:

1. Draw 2 axes on graph paper like this:
   Plot hand length and foot length
   for each child as an ordered pair.
   Put a dot. Khuram's and Laura's dots
   are shown. (19, 28.5) and (15,19).

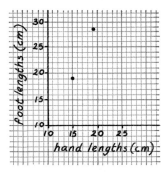

2. When you have plotted all the points,
   look how they are positioned.

   If they are clustered fairly closely
   along a diagonal, like this,
   then there is a correlation.

   If they are scattered about like this,
   there is no correlation.

3. Is there a correlation between foot
   length and hand length?

4. Find out if other pairs of measures
   correlate.

There is more about correlation on page 80.

Probability using numbers

On this spinner there are 4 segments.

The chance of spinning a blue is $\frac{2}{4}$ or $\frac{1}{2}$.

Because $\frac{1}{2}$ is equivalent to 50% and 0.5, we can say that the probability of spinning a blue is $\frac{2}{4}$ or $\frac{1}{2}$ or 50% or 0.5.

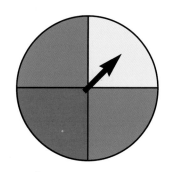

Here are 10 playing cards:

Write the probability of picking these if the cards were shuffled and placed face down.

Write your answers as fractions, percentages and decimals.

1. 7 of diamonds

2. an even number

3. a multiple of 3

4. a king

5. an odd number

6. a number which is not 5

Test your answers with a set of the same cards.

Pick a card. Write what it is. Replace it.

Shuffle the pack. Repeat.

Do the results agree with your probabilities?

Probability   Unit 1   Assigning a numerical value to probability

What is the chance?

These marbles were put into a lucky dip bag.

Write the probability of pulling these from the bag.

Use fractions, percentages and decimals.

1. a blue marble
2. a yellow marble
3. a black marble
4. a red marble
5. a blue cube
6. a green marble

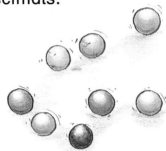

Football team record

A football team played 20 games. It won 4, lost 15 and drew 1.

Based on its record, what is the probability that it will:

7. win its next game?

8. lose its next game?

9. draw its next game?

Jane's handbag

Jane's handbag is a mess. She has 9 loose keys in it. 2 are car keys. 3 are house keys.

If she dips into her bag, what is the probability that she will pick:

10. a house key?

11. a car key?

12. neither a house key nor a car key?

There is more about probability on page 82.

Can you divide the remainder?

Sometimes if you are dividing, there are things left over.
We call these remainders.

$9 \div 2 = 4 \, r \, 1$

These 9 children were divided into 2 teams. One person was left over. You cannot divide him up.

Sometimes you can divide the remainder into smaller pieces, sometimes you can't.

 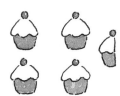

$9 \div 2 = 4.5$ cakes.

The last cake can be shared between 2 children.

Answer these division questions. Decide when to leave a remainder and when to use fractions or decimals.

1. 12 marbles between 5 children

2. 3 lettuces between 2 rabbits

3. 15 chairs between 4 people

4. 25 metres of skipping rope between 20 children

5. 40 boiled sweets between 13 children

6. 500 g of cake mix between 8 cake tins

7. 50 cows between 3 herds

8. 15 brushes between 6 artists

What will you do with the remainder?

Work out these problems in your own way. Decide when to leave a remainder and when to divide it.

1. Apples are packed into boxes of 24.
   There are 845 apples to pack.
   How many boxes are needed?

2. 375 g of cheese is cut to make 12 sandwiches. How much cheese is in each sandwich?

3. A ship travels 750 miles in a day. What is its average speed in m.p.h?

4. The pirate ship at a fair holds 42 people. How many rides are needed if there are 257 people in the queue?

5. £12.90 was left over after a school trip. It was shared equally between 29 children. How much did each child get?

There is more about remainders on page 94.

Mayan numerals

The Mayans of Central America used a number system based on dots and dashes. It is thought to be over 5000 years old.

•	• •	• • •	• • • •	——	• ——	• • ——	• • • ——	• • • • ——	—— ——
1	2	3	4	5	6	7	8	9	10

• —— ——	• • —— ——	• • • —— ——	• • • • —— ——	—— —— ——	• —— —— ——	• • —— —— ——	• • • —— —— ——	• • • • —— —— ——	•
11	12	13	14	15	16	17	18	19	20

Dots and dashes written vertically above represent twenties. The symbol is used as a space marker for zero.

$$
\left. \begin{array}{l} \bullet\bullet \quad = 2 \times 20 \\[1em] \bullet\bullet\bullet \quad = 3 \end{array} \right\} \ 43
$$

and

$$
\left. \begin{array}{l} \overset{\bullet}{——} \quad = 6 \times 20 \\[1em] \text{} \ = 0 \end{array} \right\} \ 120
$$

Which numbers do these Mayan numerals show?

1.

2.

3.

4.

5.

6.

Write these using Mayan symbols.

7. 17

8. 160

9. 314

Babylonian number system

The Babylonians used wedge shapes to represent numbers.
They wrote the numerals in damp clay using a reed with a
wedge-shaped cross-section.

Can you see how the system worked?

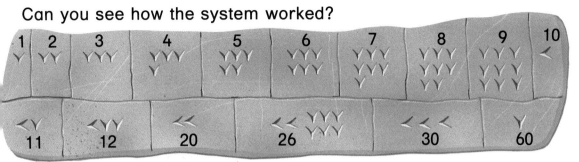

The signs for 1 and 60 were the same.
This could be confusing!

Sometimes they used this sign in their numerals V>
It means minus.

So <<Vⱽ   means 19 (20 minus 1)

   <<<<Vⱽⱽ   means 38 (40 minus 2)

Change these numerals to the Babylonian system.

1. 13   2. 18   3. 24   4. 29   5. 46

Change these numerals to our system.

6. < VVV   7. <<VV   8. Vⱽ   9. <<<<<VVV   10.V<V
     VVV   VVV
                                            V

Find out more about the Babylonians.
Try making a wedge printer using balsa wood
or a length of dowel.
Use it to print Babylonian numerals in clay
or Plasticine.

Square numbers

Remember: when you multiply a number by itself you get a square number. A square number makes a square when it is drawn as an array.

· · · ·
· · · ·
· · · ·
· · · ·

4 x 4 can be written 4^2.

4 x 4 = 16

4^2 = 16

16 is a square number.

1. Which numbers up to 100 are square numbers?

Because 16 = 4 x 4 we call 4 the square root of 16.

What is the square root of these?

2. 25   **3.** 100   **4.** 144

5. 225   **6.** 400   **7.** 10 000

8. List the odd numbers 1, 3, 5, 7 ...

Add together the first two: 1 + 3 = 4

Now add together the first three: (1 + 3 + 5),
                 the first four: (1 + 3 + 5 + 7).

And so on.
What do you notice?

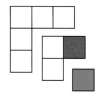

Cube numbers

Remember: a cube has its length, breadth and height all equal.

Here is a 3 x 3 x 3 cube.
It is made from 27 cubes.
3 x 3 x 3 = 27
3 x 3 x 3 can be written as 3^3 (three cubed).
So $3^3 = 27$.

What are:

1. 2^3?
2. 4^3?
3. 5^3?

Because 27 = 3 x 3 x 3 we call 3 the cube root of 27.

What are the cube roots of

4. 1000?
5. 216?
6. 1?

To find a cube root that is not exact you need to use trial and improvement.

To find the cube root of 50 correct to 2 decimal places.

Try: 3 x 3 x 3 = 27 too small
4 x 4 x 4 = 64 too big
3.6 x 3.6 x 3.6 = 46.656 too small
3.7 x 3.7 x 3.7 = 50.653 too big (just)
3.68 x 3.68 x 3.68 = 49.836
3.69 x 3.69 x 3.69 = 50.243
3.68 is closer

Use your calculator to find the cube roots of these numbers.
Correct to 2 decimal places:

7. 10
8. 100

A powerful page

Remember: 2^2 means 2 x 2
2^3 means 2 x 2 x 2

2^2 is the product of 2 equal numbers (2 x 2). The value of 2^2 ('two squared') is 4.

2^3 is the product of 3 equal numbers (2 x 2 x 2). The value of 2^3 ('two cubed') is 8.

The product of 4 equal numbers (2 x 2 x 2 x 2) is written like this: 2^4

2^4 means 2 x 2 x 2 x 2 = 16. The value of 2^4 (2 raised to the power of 4) is 16.

In this case, 2 is the base and 4 the index. 2^4

Copy and complete this chart.

	Power	Base	Index	Meaning	Numeral
1.	3^2	3	2	3 x 3	9
2.	2^4				
3.		6	3		
4.				4 x 4	
5.	10^5				
6.		3			81
7.				7 x 7 x 7	
8.		2			64

Powers of 10

Investigate powers of 10.

We say that:
$$10^0 = 1$$
$$10^1 = 10$$
$$10^2 = 10 \times 10 = 100$$
$$10^3 = 10 \times 10 \times 10 = 1000$$

Make a chart.

1.

Power	Base	Index	Numeral
10^0	10	0	1
10^1	10	1	10
	10	2	100
	10	3	
	10	4	
10^5	10	5	
	10	6	1 000 000

Numbers can be written in extended form using powers of 10.
$$356 = 3 \times 10^2 + 5 \times 10^1 + 6 \times 10^0$$

Write these numbers in extended form.

2. 5642

3. 64 172

4. 10 013

There is more about powers of 10 on page 88.

What is happening to the numbers?

Here is a decimal number function machine.

Here are some function machines with numbers or functions missing. Copy and complete them.

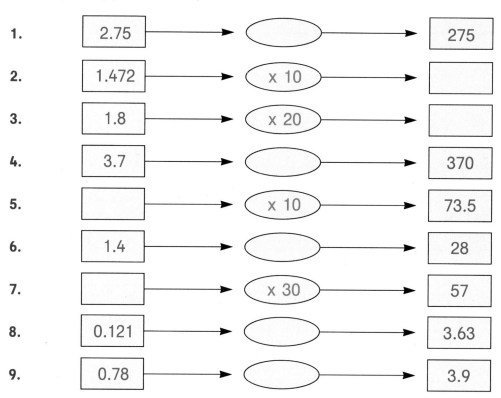

1. 2.75 → ( ) → 275

2. 1.472 → (x 10) → ☐

3. 1.8 → (x 20) → ☐

4. 3.7 → ( ) → 370

5. ☐ → (x 10) → 73.5

6. 1.4 → ( ) → 28

7. ☐ → (x 30) → 57

8. 0.121 → ( ) → 3.63

9. 0.78 → ( ) → 3.9

10. Make some for your friends.

Missing points and magic squares

In these multiplications the answers are correct.

The decimal points have been left out of the questions.
Estimate to find out where the decimal points should go.
Write out the problems correctly.

1. 214 x 74 = 158.36

2. 156 x 36 = 56.16

3. 214 x 74 = 15.836

4. 156 x 36 = 561.6

5. 214 x 74 = 1583.6

6. 156 x 36 = 5.616

7. 214 x 74 = 1.5836

8. 156 x 36 = 0.5616

In a magic square all the columns, rows and diagonals add up
to make the same number.

9.

12.5		
	7.25	
5.5		2.0

10.

64	1.28	46.08
28.16		

Make a magic decimal square for a friend to solve. You may
be able to change the 2 squares above to help you.

All the possible results

$$243 \times 176 = 42\,768$$

and $243 \times 17.6 = 4276.8$

and $243 \times 1.76 = 427.68$

Can you see the pattern of decimal numbers developing?
Continue the pattern as far as you can.
Now try different positions of the decimal point with the 243.

1. Make an organised list of all the possibilities.

2. If you use the digits 357 and 216 in decimal multiplications, find all the ways of making 77.112.

Missing numerals and decimal points

In these problems, either a numeral or a decimal point is missing.
Write them out correctly, so that they make sense.

3. $18.25 \times 10.6 = 19\,345$

4. $246 \times 4.9 = 120.54$

5. $44.85 \times 112 = 502.32$

6. $3\,\boxed{}.5 \times 2.7 = 98.55$

7. $78.7 \times 1\,\boxed{}.3 = 968.01$

8. $122.\boxed{} \times 3.25 = 398.45$

Slow animals

Remember: we can measure speed in metres per second (m/s).

Here are the speeds of some very slow animals in metres per second.

garden snail
0.013 m/s

spider
0.52 m/s

giant
tortoise
0.075 m/s

sloth 0.067 m/s

1. Put the animals in order from the fastest to the slowest.

2. How far would each animal travel in 10 seconds?

3. How far would each animal travel in 1 hour?

4. Estimate the time it would take a giant tortoise to travel the length of your room.

There is more about decimals on page 92.

Fractions, decimals and percentages

Remember: the same number can be written as a fraction, decimal or percentage.

For example, $\frac{1}{2} = 0.5 = 50\%$.

1. Copy and complete the chart.

Fraction	Decimal	Percentage
$\frac{1}{4}$	0.25	25%
$\frac{1}{5}$		20%
$\frac{1}{8}$	0.125	$12\frac{1}{2}\%$
$\frac{7}{10}$		
$\frac{1}{3}$		$33\frac{1}{3}\%$
$\frac{3}{4}$		
$\frac{4}{5}$		
	0.66	
		90%
	0.45	
		$37\frac{1}{2}\%$
		40%

2. Investigate some more fractions, decimals and percentages. Write them on a chart.

A lifestyle survey

In a school survey, sixty 11 year old children were asked some questions. Here are the results:

Do you:	% answered yes
go to bed before 10 pm?	$33\frac{1}{3}\%$
watch more than 2 hours TV per day?	75%
have your own door key?	25%
own a pet?	60%
go abroad for holidays?	40%
have a brother or sister?	85%
have a family car?	90%
use a computer at home?	50%

What percentage of children:

1. watch less than 2 hours TV?

2. do not own a pet?

3. have a computer at home?

4. go to bed after 10 p.m?

What fraction of children:

5. have their own door key?

6. do not have brothers or sisters?

7. have a family car?

8. go abroad for holidays?

How many children:

9. go to bed before 10 p.m? 10. own a pet?

Do a similar school survey and work out the percentages.

The golden rectangle

Some rectangles are particularly pleasing to look at. They are often used in picture frames and in architecture. They are called golden rectangles.

The ancient Greeks designed some of their buildings around the golden rectangle.

To draw a golden rectangle:

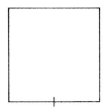 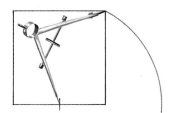 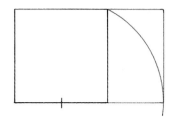

First draw a square and find the point halfway along its base.

Set your compasses from that point to the top right-hand corner of the square. Draw an arc.

Extend the base of the square to cut the arc. This is the bottom right-hand corner of the golden rectangle. Draw in the rest.

1. On a piece of A4 paper draw a 10 cm square. Extend the base and make a golden rectangle using the method shown.

Now do the same for these squares.

2. 5 cm   3. 8 cm   4. 4 cm

The golden ratio

Look at the golden rectangle you have made from a 10 cm square.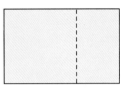

It has a length of 16.2 cm and a breadth of 10 cm. The ratio of length: breadth is 16.2:10. This is the same as 1.62:1.

1. What is the length of a golden rectangle based on a 5 cm square?

2. What is the ratio of length:breadth?

3. What is the length of a golden rectangle based on an 8 cm square?

4. What is the ratio of length:breadth?

5. What is the length of a golden rectangle based on a 4 cm square?

6. What is the ratio of length:breadth?

7. What is the ratio of length:breadth of any golden rectangle? This is known as the golden ratio.

8. Look at the piece added to a square to make a golden rectangle. What is special about the shape of this piece?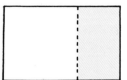

There is more about the golden ratio on page 100.

Equivalent fraction wheels

Remember: to convert a fraction to a decimal
divide the numerator by the denominator.
For example, $\frac{1}{4} = 1 \div 4 = 0.25$.

This is a fraction wheel for $\frac{1}{2}$. It shows equivalent fractions and decimals. There are other fractions which could go on this wheel, for example, $\frac{10}{20}$, $\frac{8}{16}$ or $\frac{50}{100}$.

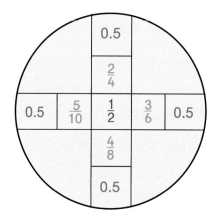

Make a wheel for each of these unitary fractions: (we call them unitary because they have 1 as the numerator).

1. $\frac{1}{4}$ 2. $\frac{1}{5}$ 3. $\frac{1}{8}$ 4. $\frac{1}{10}$

Now try these non-unitary fractions.

5. $\frac{3}{4}$ 6. $\frac{2}{5}$ 7. $\frac{3}{10}$

8. Make wheels for $\frac{1}{3}$ and $\frac{1}{6}$. What do you notice about the decimal?

Terminating and recurring decimals

Remember: some decimals terminate and some recur.

For example, when you convert $\frac{1}{2}$ to 0.5, the decimal terminates (goes no further).

But when you convert $\frac{1}{3}$, you get a recurring decimal because 0.3333333 goes on and on.

We write the recurring decimal as $0.\bar{3}$ (with a bar above the part that repeats.)

Fraction	Decimal
$\frac{1}{2}$	0.5
$\frac{1}{3}$	$0.\bar{3}$
$\frac{1}{4}$	0.25
$\frac{1}{5}$	0.2
$\frac{1}{6}$	
$\frac{1}{7}$	

1. Carry on with this chart. Add some more fractions and decimals.

2. Which fractions produce recurring decimals?

3. What do you notice about the denominators of terminating decimals and of recurring decimals?

Fraction and decimal patterns

Look at this sequence of fractions.
It is made by doubling the denominator each time.

$\frac{1}{2}$ $\frac{1}{4}$ $\frac{1}{8}$ $\frac{1}{16}$ $\frac{1}{32}$

1. Convert the fractions in the sequence to decimals.
   Record your results.
   Can you describe the pattern the decimals make?

Continue these fraction sequences as far as you like and convert them to decimals.
Describe how the fraction and decimal patterns are developing.

2. $\frac{1}{8}$ $\frac{2}{8}$ $\frac{3}{8}$ $\frac{4}{8}$

3. $\frac{1}{7}$ $\frac{2}{7}$ $\frac{3}{7}$ $\frac{4}{7}$

4. $\frac{1}{2}$ $\frac{2}{3}$ $\frac{3}{4}$ $\frac{4}{5}$ $\frac{5}{6}$

Interesting decimals

Some fraction sequences produce interesting patterns when they are converted to decimals.

For example, $\frac{1}{9}$, $\frac{2}{9}$, $\frac{3}{9}$, and so on.

$1 \div 9 = 0.1111111$

1. Continue the sequence and describe the decimals produced.

2. Now try $\frac{1}{11}$, $\frac{2}{11}$, $\frac{3}{11}$, and so on.

3. Look for more fractions that produce an interesting decimal pattern.

4. Try fractions with large denominators such as $\frac{1}{99}$, $\frac{2}{99}$, and so on.

Investigating dots and lines

If you have 2 dots, they can be joined by 1 line.

3 dots can have 3 lines.

4 dots can have 6 lines.

dots	lines
2	1
3	3
4	6

Carry on with the investigation. Keep a chart. Make a graph of your results. Use the numbers of the dots and lines as the x and y co-ordinates (2,1) (3,3) (4,6), and so on.

1. Use your graph to predict how many lines can join 10 dots.

2. Describe the line your graph makes.

Patterns with squares

These patterns can be made with tiles or on squared paper.

  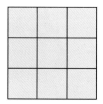 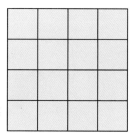

3. Continue the pattern.

4. Keep a chart of the squares (or tiles) used.

5. Draw a graph to show how the pattern grows.

Making graphs from function machines

Here are 2 function machines. They use the same numbers, but different operations.

input	function x 2 −10	output
7	⟶	4
5	⟶	0

input	function x 2 +10	output
7	⟶	24
5	⟶	20

1. Put some more numbers through these function machines.

2. Draw 2 graphs using the same axes.
   Let the x axis show the inputs and the y axis the outputs.
   Use a different colour for each function.

3. Compare your 2 graphs. What do you notice?

4. Imagine a function machine which uses 'add 2 then multiply by 10'. Make up some inputs and outputs for it.
   Plot the results, in a new colour on the same axes as your graphs in question 2. Compare your new graph with the other 2 lines.
   What do you notice?

5. Predict what will happen with the function 'multiply by 10 then add 2'. Check to see if you are right.

Running a marathon

Martin runs 200 m in 41 seconds.

1. How many metres/second is this? Write your answer correct to 2 decimal places.

2. At this speed how long will it take him to run a kilometre?

3. How long will it take him to run a marathon (42.2 kilometres)?

Ingrid Kristiansen has run a marathon in 2 hrs 21 min.

4. How many seconds is this?

5. How long did each kilometre take? Write your answer in minutes and seconds to the nearest second.

6. How fast is this in metres/second?

7. How long would 200 metres take at this speed?

Thermometer scales

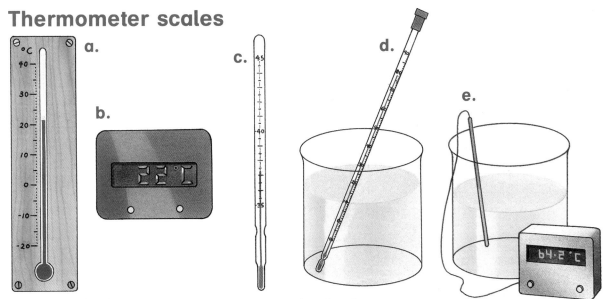

a. is used to measure temperature in the house or garden.

1. What 2 points does the temperature lie between?
2. What does the thermometer read to 2 significant figures?

b. is used to measure the temperature outside.

Write to 3 significant figures:

3. The lowest temperature this could represent.
4. The highest temperature this could represent.

c. is used to measure body temperature.

5. What is the smallest change in temperature it measures?

d. is used to measure the temperature of fluids.

6. Estimate the temperature to 3 significant figures.

e. is also used to measure the temperature of fluids.

Write to 4 significant figures:

7. The lowest the temperature could be.
8. The highest the temperature could be.

Kites

1. Measure all the sides.
   What do you notice?

2. Measure all the angles.
   What do you notice?

3. Draw a kite and mark any lines of symmetry.

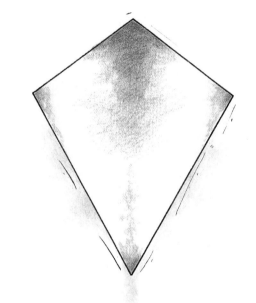

4. Draw a parallelogram. Cut it out. Cut along one of the diagonals. Use the 2 pieces to make a kite – sketch it.

   Now draw an identical parallelogram and cut along the other diagonal. Use the 2 pieces to make a kite. Sketch it.

Compare the 2 kites. What is the same and what is different?

Arrowheads

This special quadrilateral is called an arrowhead.

It has an angle which goes back into the shape

(a re-entrant angle).

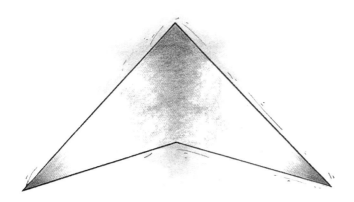

1. Measure all the sides. What do you notice?

2. Measure all the angles. What do you notice?

3. Draw an arrowhead and mark any lines of symmetry.

4. Draw a parallelogram. Cut it out and cut along the short diagonal. Use the 2 pieces to make an arrowhead. Sketch it. Now use the same 2 pieces to make a different arrowhead. Sketch it.

Compare the 2 arrowheads. What is the same and what is different?

Investigating angles and drawing kites

1. Copy this kite. Draw in the diagonals.

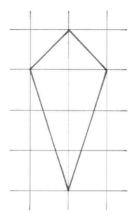

2. Describe the angles where the diagonals cross.

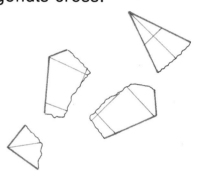

3. Draw another kite the same.
    Cut it out.
    Tear off the 4 vertices.
    Put them together.
    What is the sum of the angles?

Draw kites with these diagonals:

4. 4 cm and 6 cm

5. 3 cm and 7 cm

6. 5 cm and 9 cm

7. 2 cm and 8 cm

Making kites and arrowheads

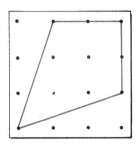

| You will need a geoboard. |

1. Sketch the different kites you can make on a 4 x 4 geoboard.

2. Sketch the different arrowheads you can make on a 4 x 4 geoboard.

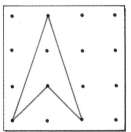

3. Draw an arrowhead like this one:

   Draw in the diagonals.

   What do you notice?

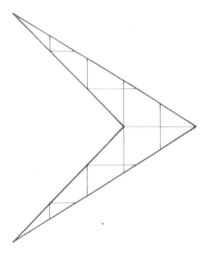

Draw arrowheads with these diagonals:

4. 4 cm and 6 cm

5. 3 cm and 7 cm

Name the view

Remember: objects change in appearance as they are viewed
from different directions. Designers use different
views to help them portray three-dimensional objects.

From these photographs say whether the view is from the front,
back, side, top or bottom:

1.

2.

3.

4.

5.

6.

Name the view and the object.

7.

8.

9.

Drawing plans

Draw an accurate front view, side view and top view
for each shape.

1.

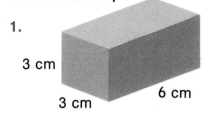

3 cm

3 cm

6 cm

2.

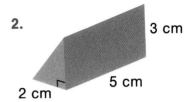

3 cm

2 cm

5 cm

3.

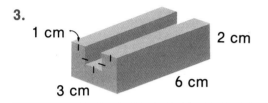

1 cm

2 cm

3 cm

6 cm

4. Make this model from cubes.
   Accurately draw a top view, side view and front view.
   Give your drawings to a friend and ask him or her to make
   the model.

5. Make a different model of your own. Draw it from 3 different
   views to help a friend construct an identical model.

Rotating squares ...

You will need card, scissors and squared paper.

1. Cut out a 4 cm x 4 cm square from card. Find the centre of the square. Write A, B, C and D in each of the corners.

   Place the card on squared paper and draw its outline. Write A, B, C or D in the correct corners.

   Turn the card clockwise through one right angle. Draw the outline and write the new positions of the letters.
   Continue until the card returns to the starting position.

   The centre of the square is known as the centre of rotation.

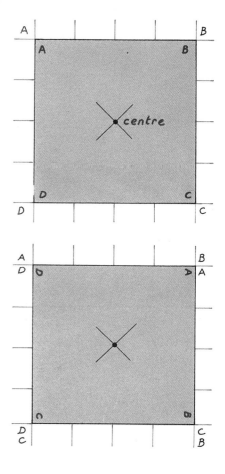

2. Do the same, but this time rotate the square anti-clockwise. What happens to the order of the letters?

3. Rotate the square around one of its corners. Stop each time you have rotated through one right angle and trace around the square.

4. Now do the same, but stop after each half right angle (45°).

... and other shapes

1. Cut a rectangle out of card. Draw an outline of it on a piece of paper. On the rectangle mark where its diagonals cross. Now use a pin to rotate the rectangle one right angle around this point. Draw an outline of the rectangle in the new position. Continue rotating through a right angle and drawing around the rectangle until you return to the original position. Describe the shape you have created.

2. Repeat the procedure, but this time rotate the rectangle around one of its vertices. Describe the shape you create.

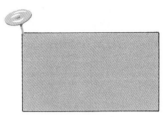

3. Now cut out an equilateral triangle and draw its outline. Rotate it around one of its vertices. Stop and draw an outline each time you turn through a right angle.

   Describe the shape you create.

4. Repeat what you did in question **3**. But this time stop and draw again as soon as the card triangle stops overlapping the original shape.

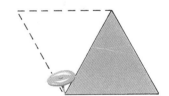

   What shape have you created?

   How many triangles will you need to draw to get right round?

   What shape is created?

   Try these ideas on the computer using LOGO.

There is more about rotation on page 110.

Different triangles

When we describe triangles we can talk about their angles or the length of their sides.

An acute-angled triangle has all its angles less than a right angle. (90°).

A right-angled triangle has one angle of 90°.

An obtuse-angled triangle has one angle greater than a right angle.

For each of these triangles say whether it is acute, right or obtuse-angled.

1.   2.   3.   4.

5. A triangle with no sides the same length is called scalene.

6. A triangle with 2 sides the same length is called isosceles.

7. A triangle with 3 sides the same length is called equilateral.

For each of these triangles say whether it is scalene, isosceles or equilateral:

5.   6.   7.   8.

What's the angle?

Cut out a paper triangle. Tear off the vertices
and put them together.

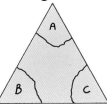

You will find the angles add up to a straight line, so the sum of the
angles is 180°.

Measure the angles on these triangles carefully.

1.　　　　　　　**2.**　　　　　　　**3.**

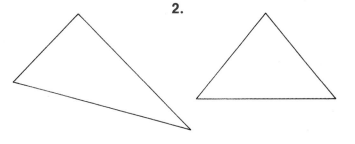

Check that they each total 180°.

Calculate the size of the angle marked 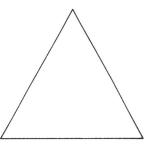 in each of
these drawings.

4.　　　　　　**5.**　　　　　　**6.**

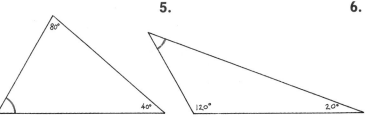　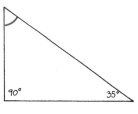

7.　　　　　　**8.**　　　　　　**9.**

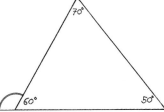　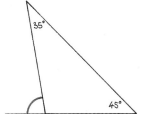　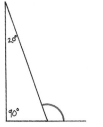

Surveying lengths of words

> Remember: the median is the middle number in an ordered set of data.
> If there are 2 middle numbers, it is the mean of these 2 numbers.

This frequency table shows the result of Harprit's survey of 50 words in his library book.

He had counted the number of letters in each word.

How many letters were there in:

Harprit's Book		
Number of Letters	Tally	Frequency
1	III	3
2	IIII II	7
3	IIII IIII	10
4	IIII IIII I	11
5	IIII II	7
6	IIII II	7
7	III	3
8	I	1
11	I	1

1. the longest word?

2. the shortest word?

3. Write down the range of letters per word.

4. What was the mode (most common) size of word?

5. What was the median word size?

6. How many letters did Harprit count in total?

   Use this information to calculate the mean number of letters per word.

Comparing books

Anne also did a survey of her library book. Here are her 50 words.

> Then John answered, 'I am a merchant,' and opening his napkin, he showed her its contents. Then she exclaimed, 'Oh, what beautiful golden things!' and, setting the pails down, she looked at the cups one after another and said, 'The king's daughter must see these; she is so pleased with anything.........

1. Make a frequency table like the one on page 78.

   Use your table to answer these questions.

What is:

2. the range of word lengths?

3. the mode size of word?

4. the median size of word?

5. the mean size of word?

6. Whose book would you say has the longest words, Harprit's or Anne's?

   Say why you think this.

You might like to compare your library book with your friend's in the same way.

Test results

Name	Maths Score %	Spelling out of 20	Reading Age	Science Test out of 20
Khuram	91	20	12.3	12
Laura	82	18	10.9	18
Kelly	77	14	9.7	9
Nick	96	20	13.2	20
Russell	84	17	11.3	11
Anita	67	17	10.6	15
Melanie	71	18	10.9	15
Ian	78	19	11.7	16
Emma	65	16	8.6	18
Umeed	97	19	12.1	13
Hitesh	75	16	10.8	6
Jenny	42	6	6.3	9
Kathleen	74	13	9.4	8
Martin	83	17	10.7	5
Simon	89	20	13.4	17
Ricki	48	12	9.5	18
Kerry	55	18	11.3	20
Yasmin	74	18	10.7	10
Tony	92	20	12.5	6
Anita	61	9	8.7	4
Fawad	82	18	11.1	15
Amy	75	14	10.5	12
Robyn	32	4	5.6	15
Angela	68	20	11.2	13
Simran	81	20	10.7	20
Tom	79	15	12.8	4
Paul	54	8	7.5	13
Vijay	65	17	10.5	2
Balbir	73	19	11.7	19
Jamie	62	16	9.8	9

Class correlations

Remember: a scatter diagram is used to see if there is a correlation (relationship) between 2 sets of data.

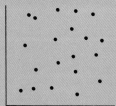

This scatter diagram shows that there is a correlation.

This scatter diagram shows no correlation.

Use the database on page 80 to draw scatter diagrams to find out if there is a correlation between:

1. maths score and reading age

2. spelling score and reading age

3. maths score and science score

4. Choose one of these to investigate.
   Survey your class.
   Draw a scatter diagram to see if there is a correlation between:

The amount of pocket money a child gets and how tall he/she is.

The height of children and the time it takes them to run 100 metres.

The cost of a potato snack and its weight.

Hand area and foot area.

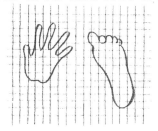

Weather predictions

The number of days of rainfall during the first week of May for a 20 year period is shown in the table.

Days of Rain: First Week of May			
1965	1	1975	2
1966	3	1976	4
1967	4	1977	0
1968	2	1978	1
1969	2	1979	2
1970	3	1980	2
1971	2	1981	4
1972	6	1982	1
1973	2	1983	2
1974	5	1984	3

Here is a way of organising the information:

	Number of Years
No rain (0 days)	1
'Little rain' (1 or 2 days)	11
'Some rain' (3 or 4 days)	6
'Lots of rain' (5 or 6 days)	2

Based on the information, it is most likely that there will be 'little rain' during the first week of May next year.

We had 'little rain' in 11 out of 20 years. We can say that the probability of 'little rain' is $\frac{11}{20}$. This is 55%

In fractions and percentages, what is the probability of:

1. no rain?

2. some rain?

3. a lot of rain?

4. What are we least likely to have in the first week of May?

A probability game

In this game a marble is rolled down a ramp.

On the way down, it hits several pins.
At each pin, it can turn right or left,
until it reaches one of
the holes at the bottom.

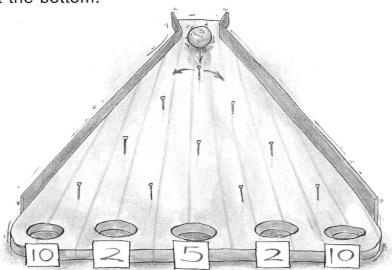

Investigate how many routes there are to reach:

1. 10   2. 5   3. 2

4. How many possible routes are there altogether?

With one marble, what is the probability of scoring:

5. 10?   6. 5?   7. 2?

8. Use a piece of board and some nails to make a similar game.

   Use the probabilities of your game to predict approximately
   how many times each number would be scored if you rolled
   a marble 50 times.
   Test your predictions.

There is more about probability on page 124.

Find the pairs

In this grid some pairs of numbers add up to make 1000, some pairs make 2000 and some pairs make 5000.

462	856	3836	262
658	819	1144	959
1254	1164	191	1071
2646	4041	929	738
538	3746	1342	2354

1. Write the pairs and their sums, for example 462 + 538 = 1000. Try to estimate first. Do them in your head or with pencil and paper.

2. Make up a grid like this for a friend to try.

Brain power

Some people have astounding abilities for mental calculations.

Mrs Shakuntala Devi multiplied 7 686 369 774 870 by 2 465 099 745 779 correctly in 28 seconds.

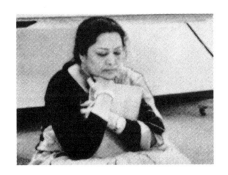

These examples show some ways to group or write numbers to make mental calculations easier.

$$19 + 52 + 28$$

$$19 + 52 + 28$$
$$= 19 + (52 + 28)$$
$$= 19 + 80$$
$$= 99$$

> Group into multiples of 10.

$$6 \times 14 \times 5$$

$$6 \times 14 \times 5$$
$$= (6 \times 5) \times 14$$
$$= 30 \times 14$$
$$= 420$$

$$72 \times 102$$

$$102 = 100 + 2$$
So 72×102
$$= 72 \times (100 + 2)$$
$$= 72 \times 100 + 72 \times 2$$
$$= 7200 + 144$$
$$= 7344$$

> Write as a multiple of 10 and a single digit.

$$19 \times 43$$

$$19 = 20 - 1$$
So 19×43
$$= (20 - 1) \times 43$$
$$= 20 \times 43 - 1 \times 43$$
$$= 860 - 43$$
$$= 817$$

Which numbers could be grouped to make mental calculations easier?

1. $43 + 76 + 224$

2. $11 \times 18 \times 5$

3. $79 + 82 + 21$

4. $15 \times 7 \times 6$

Try to work out the answers to these mentally.

5. $25 \times 71 \times 4$

6. $31 \times 45 \times 0$

7. $11 + 45 + 49$

8. 48×101

9. $92 - 58 - 32$

10. 99×8

Modern number systems

Our present numeral system is a base 10 system. It has 10 digits and is based on powers of 10.

The 10 digits are: 0 1 2 3 4 5 6 7 8 9

We use them to make big numbers by giving them place value.

This chart shows the value of 25 847.

2	5	8	4	7
ten thousands 10 000 (10 x 10 x 10 x 10) 10^4	thousands 1000 (10 x 10 x 10) 10^3	hundreds 100 (10 x 10) 10^2	tens 10 (1 x 10) 10^1	ones 1 10^0

In expanded form 25 847 can be written:
$(2 \times 10^3) + (5 \times 10^3) + (8 \times 10^2) + (4 \times 10^1) + (7 \times 10^0)$

Make a chart for these numbers and then write them in expanded form.

1. 6437

2. 19 782

3. 75 168

4. 436

5. 2981

6. 85 657

Now look at the binary system on page 87.

The binary system

There is a numeral system that only uses 2 digits. It is called the binary system. The digits used are 1 and 0 and the place values are powers of 2.

$$2^0 = 1 \qquad 2^1 = 2 \qquad 2^2 = 2 \times 2 = 4 \qquad 2^3 = 2 \times 2 \times 2 = 8$$

$$2^4 = 2 \times 2 \times 2 \times 2 = 16 \qquad 2^5 = 2 \times 2 \times 2 \times 2 \times 2 = 32$$

You can still make all the other numbers if you use a chart like this:

$\begin{array}{c}32\\2^5\end{array}$	$\begin{array}{c}16\\2^4\end{array}$	$\begin{array}{c}8\\2^3\end{array}$	$\begin{array}{c}4\\2^2\end{array}$	$\begin{array}{c}2\\2^1\end{array}$	$\begin{array}{c}1\\2^0\end{array}$
				1	1
		1	0	1	1
1	0	1	1	0	1

11 represents 3 (2 + 1)
1011 represents 11 (8 + 2 + 1)
101101 represents 45 (32 + 8 + 4 + 1)

Make a chart and write these as binary numerals.
Remember to only use 0 and 1.

1. 7
2. 15
3. 22
4. 8
5. 56
6. 35
7. 16
8. 42
9. What is the next column in the binary chart?
10. Write your age in binary.

The power of big numbers

Remember: numbers can be written in different ways:
ordinary numeral 53862
expanded form $(5 \times 10000) + (3 \times 1000) + (8 \times 100) + (6 \times 10) + (2 \times 1)$
They can also be written using powers of 10:
$(5 \times 10^4) + (3 \times 10^3) + (8 \times 10^2) + (6 \times 10^1) + (2 \times 10^0)$

Write these numbers out as ordinary numerals, in expanded form and as powers of 10.

1. three thousand, four hundred and seventy-two

2. sixteen thousand, four hundred and eighty-seven

3. two hundred and forty-three

4. one hundred and five thousand, nine hundred and twenty-five

5. one million, three hundred and sixty-two thousand, four hundred and sixty-eight

6. the current year

Powers and prime factors

Remember: to find the prime factors of a number you can use
a factor tree.

The prime factors of 36 look like this
on a factor tree.

The prime factors are 2 x 2 x 3 x 3
= 36

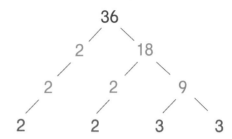

The prime factors of 36 can be written using powers: $2^2 \times 3^2 = 36$

Write the prime factors for these number trees. They have been
started for you. Write the prime factors using powers.

1.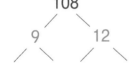

2.

Draw factor trees and write the prime factors as powers for these
numbers:

3. 99   4. 60   5. 125

6. 100   7. 64   8. 288

9. Do the same, but choose your own numbers. Ask a friend to
   check them.

Negative number patterns

If you continue to subtract when you reach zero (0), negative numbers will begin to appear:

$9 - 5 = 4$
$9 - 6 = 3$
$9 - 7 = 2$
$9 - 8 = 1$
$9 - 9 = 0$
$9 - 10 = -1$
$9 - 11 = -2$

Copy and continue these patterns. What is the 10th number in each one?

You could check with a calculator.

1. $5 - 2 = 3$
   $5 - 3 = 2$
   $5 - 4 = 1$

2. $12 - 6 = 6$
   $12 - 7 = 5$
   $12 - 8 = 4$

3. $10 - 7 = 3$
   $10 - 8 = 2$
   $10 - 9 = 1$

4. $8 - 2 = 6$
   $6 - 2 = 4$
   $4 - 2 = 2$

5. $25 - 5 = 20$
   $20 - 5 = 15$
   $15 - 5 = 10$

6. $11 - 3 = 8$
   $8 - 3 = 5$
   $5 - 3 = 2$

$3 - 5 = -2$

The difference between 3 and -2 is 5.

Find the difference between these pairs of numbers.
A number line may help you.

7. 1 and -5

8. 7 and -7

9. -2 and -10

10. -8 and -25

Magic squares

−3	+2	−5
−4	−2	0
+1	−6	−1

This magic square uses positive and negative numbers. Each column, row and diagonal adds up to −6.

Copy and complete these magic squares:

1.

−11	−6	−13
		−9

2.

−1		
	0	
+3		+1

3.

−8	−4	0
+2		

4.

		−8
	−2	+2
+14		

5. Make up your own magic squares using positive and negative numbers. The ones above may help you. Give yours to a friend to work out.

What divides easily?

£3.99	£5.25	£8.48	£24.08
£4.16	£10.20	£5.55	£4.24
£15.75	£12.33	£6.36	£10.50
£3.12	£9.63	£20.10	£16.04

Remember: on page 9 there are some quick ways of seeing if a number can be divided by 3, 4 or 5.

Do these in your head.

Write the amounts of money which are **easily** shared.

1. between 3.

2. between 4.

3. between 5.

Now work these out in your head.

4. £12.72 ÷ 6

5. £4.44 ÷ 2

6. £4.48 ÷ 4

7. £3.33 ÷ 3

8. £5.50 ÷ 5

9. £12.60 ÷ 6

The sawmill

The sawmill will cut pieces of wood to any length.
They start off with planks 5 metres long.

How long would each piece be:

1. If they cut a plank into 4 pieces?

2. If they cut a plank in half?

3. How many planks would be needed to cut 6 pieces, each 2.5 metres long?

4. A plank was cut into 8 equal pieces. 5 pieces were sold. How long was all the wood left over?

5. 8 planks were cut into 0.5 m lengths. How many pieces of wood did this give?

What will you do with the remainder?

> Remember: you only divide a remainder if it makes sense to do so.
> Sometimes there really is an amount left over that will not be used, this should be shown as a remainder.

Solve these problems. Decide whether it is sensible to divide the remainder. Write the answers. Decide how many decimal places you will use.

1. A carpet layer has a huge roll of stair carpet 250 m long. He cuts it into 15 m lengths. How many does he get?

2. A light aircraft flies 257 miles using 78 l of fuel. How many miles does it travel for each litre?

3. 2.5 m of ribbon is cut into 16 pieces. How long is each piece?

4. How many ribbons 16 cm long can be cut from a length of 2.5 m?

5. £75 is divided equally between 4 people. How much will each person get?

Value for money

To test value for money, you need to work out the unit cost.
The unit cost is the cost of one item.

A pack of 24 envelopes costs £1.25.

To find the cost of one envelope (the unit cost), we divide the price of the pack by the number in the pack. It is easiest to use a calculator for this.

£1.25 ÷ 24 = £0.0520833

price ÷ number = unit cost

You cannot actually have £0.0520833. We don't have coins small enough!
Only the first 2 decimal figures, £0.05, are significant.
They stand for 5p.
In this case it is sensible to give the answer (the unit cost) as about £0.05 or 5p.
Here is a selection of greetings cards. List them in order of best value for money. Write the unit cost for each pack.

Number in pack	Theme	Pack price
12	Sports	£1.99
24	Flowers	£3.45
36	Assorted	£5.49
12	Woodland Tales	£2.29
8	Nursery Rhymes	£1.95
8	Hobbies	£1.39
10	Country Scenes	£1.85
15	Alpine Scenes	£3.15

Doing Europe

Two American friends decided to tour around Europe.
They started in Britain with $2000 (2000 US dollars).

This chart shows the currency exchange rates, that is,
how much of each sort of money you can buy for £1.

Country	£1 is worth	Currency
Austria	16.98	schillings
Belgium	49.62	Belgian francs
Denmark	9.31	Danish krone
France	8.26	French francs
Germany	2.41	Deutschmarks
Italy	2105	lira
Netherlands	2.71	guilders
Portugal	216.88	escudos
Spain	173.4	pesetas
Sweden	10.34	Swedish krona
Switzerland	2.18	Swiss francs
U.S.A.	1.5	U.S. dollars

Changing money

Write the answers to these in the nearest whole unit of currency.

1. When they arrived in Britain, how many pounds did they exchange their dollars for?

2. They bought souvenirs in London for £125. How much money did they have left?

3. How many French francs did this buy them?

4. In France they spent 550 francs. How much did they have left?

5. In Germany, they changed their francs into Deutschmarks. How many Deutschmarks did they get?

6. They hired a car for 2 days and went skiing. They spent 675 Deutschmarks. How much did they have left?

7. They decided to spend a week sunbathing in Spain. How many pesetas did they get for their Deutschmarks?

8. They spent 85000 pesetas. How much did they have left?

9. When they got home, they converted their pesetas back to U.S. dollars. How much did they get?

Finding percentages

Remember: percent means 'out of 100'. So 50% means 50 out of every 100.

When working out a percentage of an amount, it is sometimes helpful to convert it to a fraction. For example,

10% of 50 is similar to saying

$\frac{1}{10}$ of 50 which is 5.

Write how much these percentages represent.

1. 50% of £2.50
2. 25% of 4 kg
3. 75% of 1 litre
4. 10% of 80
5. 5% of £1.60
6. 45% of 900 g
7. 75% of one day
8. $33\frac{1}{3}$ % of 30 cm
9. 90% of 100 m
10. 15% of 120

11. An animal charity appeal collected £2004.80. The money was shared in this way.

25% to the Cat Sanctuary

40% to the Dogs' Home

20% to the Donkey Rescue

15% to the Hawk Conservancy

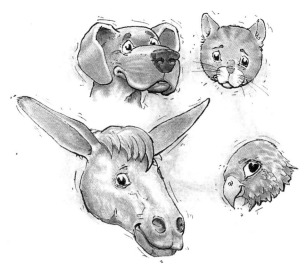

How much did each charity receive?

Dealing with discounts

Sometimes when shops have sales they show the reduction in price as a percentage discount. For example, 25% off means that each price is reduced by 25% or $\frac{1}{4}$. (You pay 75% or $\frac{3}{4}$ of the original price.)

1. Copy and complete the chart.

Old Price	Percentage discount	Money off	New Price
£75	10%	£7.50	£67.50
£40	5%	£2.00	
£52		£5.20	
£125			£100.00
£60		£30.00	
£245	20%		
£339		£113.00	
£850	25%		
£1260	15%		
£2612			£2481.40

2. Collect discount advertisements from newspapers and check that the percentage discounts are correct.

Drawing a golden ratio spiral

Remember: the golden ratio is the ratio of length: breadth of a particularly pleasing rectangle called the golden rectangle. The golden ratio is approximately 1.62:1

In nature there are many spirals. Ferns, snail shells, butterflies' tongues and even storm systems are spiral in shape. Some of these follow the golden ratio. One particularly beautiful sea snail called the Nautilus has a shell with chambers which get larger according to the golden ratio.

You can draw a golden spiral.

1. Start with a square and extend it to a golden rectangle. See page 58 if you can't remember how.

2. Mark off a square in the small golden rectangle.

3. Carry on marking off squares as you produce new golden rectangles.

4. Draw arcs across the squares to produce a spiral.

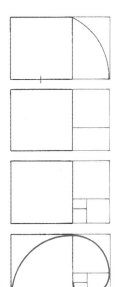

The golden ratio in numbers

The golden ratio appears in all sorts of places.

1. Measure your height as accurately as you can.
   Now measure the height of your navel.
   What is the ratio of these 2 heights?

   Do the same with several friends and find the average ratio.
   Measured accurately to 3 decimal places the golden ratio
   is 1.618:1.

   The Fibonacci series 1, 1, 2, 3, 5, 8, 13, 21 is formed by adding
   2 consecutive numbers to get the next number.

2. Divide consecutive numbers in the Fibonacci series,
   e.g. $1 \div 1$, $2 \div 1$, $3 \div 2$, $5 \div 3$.
   Carry on. What do you find?

Taking the golden ratio as 1.618, find correct to 3 decimal places:

3. $1 \div$ golden ratio

4. $(\text{golden ratio})^2$

5. golden ratio
   x
   (golden ratio -1)

6. (golden ratio -1)
   x
   (golden ratio $+ 1$)

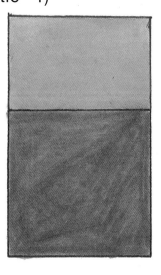

Spreadsheets and tables above 10

Remember: a spreadsheet is a chart.

A computer spreadsheet will do all the working out for you.
All it needs to know is what to do to each column.
To tell it, you need to put a formula (instruction) at the top
of each column.

1. This spreadsheet will list multiplication tables for some of the
   numbers above 10. In the first column, marked 'A', are the
   numbers from 1 to 8. The other columns will multiply each
   number by 11, 12 etc. Copy it and fill in the missing numbers.

A	A x 11	A x 12	A x 13	A x 14	A x 15
1	11	12	13	14	
2	22	24	26		
3	33	36			
4	44				
5					
6					
7					
8					

2. Create this spreadsheet on a computer to make a ready
   reckoner for multiplication tables above 10.

More about spreadsheets

Remember: when a number is raised to a power, the power
shows the number of times it is multiplied by itself.
3^4 is 3 raised to the power 4.
3^4 means 3 x 3 x 3 x 3.

1. Copy and continue this spreadsheet which shows powers.

A	A^2 A x A	A^3 A x A x A	A^4 A x A x A x A
1	1	1	1
2	4	8	
3	9		

2. If possible, try this spreadsheet on a computer.

3. Design a spreadsheet to investigate the pattern of decimal
   numbers produced by the sevenths, $\frac{1}{7}$, $\frac{2}{7}$, $\frac{3}{7}$ etc.
   Put 1, 2, 3 ... down the cells on the first column, put 7 in each
   cell of the second column, and put a formula to divide them in
   the third column. Now look at $\frac{1}{13}$, $\frac{2}{13}$ etc.

Volume and surface area

This cube has edges 1 cm long.
It has a surface area of 6 cm^2.
It has a volume of 1 cm^3.

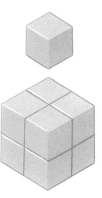

This cube has edges 2 cm long.
It has a surface area of 24 cm^2.
It has a volume of 8 cm^3.

1. Design a spreadsheet which compares lengths of side, surface areas and volumes of cubes. Here is the start.

length of side	surface area	volume
1 cm	6 cm^2	1 cm^3
2 cm	24 cm^2	8 cm^3
3 cm		
4 cm		
5 cm		

2. Put your spreadsheet on to the computer. You will need to work out a formula for the head of each column.

Guess the formula

In this spreadsheet the formula for column B is B = 2 x A

A	B	C	D	E	F
1	2	1	6	1.5	30
2	4	4	8	2	40
3	6	9	10	2.5	50
4	8	16	12	3	60
5	10	25	14	3.5	70
6	12	36	16	4	80

What is the formula for   1. C   2. D   3. E   4. F

Make up a column and ask a friend to work out the formula.

Scale drawing

Remember: when drawing to scale every length is reduced by the same scale factor. If 1 metre is represented by 2 cm, then all lines are reduced to $\frac{1}{50}$ of their real length.

Measure the shadow of the metre stick and the shadow of the tree.

1. How tall is the tree?

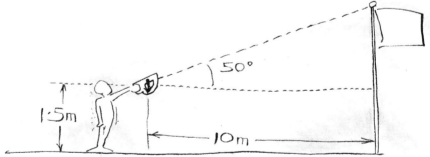

A clinometer measures angles up from the horizontal.

2. This is a sketch drawn whilst using a clinometer.
   Make an accurate scale drawing.
   How tall is the flagpole?

Paper prisms

Remember: the volume of a prism may be calculated by
multiplying the area of an end face by the length.

Give your answers in cm, cm^2 or cm^3 to 2 significant
figures.

Fold a piece of A4 paper this way:
Make a square prism without ends.

1. How long is the prism?

2. What is the length of side of the square?

3. What is the area of the square?

4. Now work out the volume of the prism?

Now fold a piece of A4 paper this way:

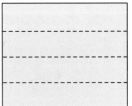

5. Work out the volume of the square prism.

Fold A4 paper to make a triangular prism.

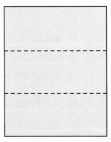

6. How long is the prism?

7. What is the area of its triangular face?

8. Now work out the volume of the triangular prism?

Special quadrilaterals

Remember: a quadrilateral is a shape with 4 sides;
a parallelogram is a quadrilateral with 2 pairs of parallel sides;
a rhombus is a parallelogram with all 4 sides equal;
a rectangle is a parallelogram with right angles;
a square is a parallelogram with 4 equal sides and right angles;
a trapezium is a quadrilateral with just one pair of parallel sides;
a kite is a quadrilateral with 2 pairs of adjacent (next to) sides equal;
an arrowhead is a quadrilateral with 2 pairs of adjacent sides equal, and a re-entrant angle.

Copy this 5 piece tangram on to card and cut out the pieces.

Use 2 of the pieces to make:

1. a square
2. another parallelogram
3. a trapezium

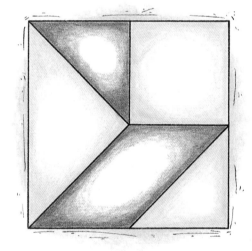

Use 3 of the pieces to make:

4. a square
5. a rectangle whose length is twice its width.
6. a trapezium

Sketch the shapes you have made to show which pieces you used.

Experiment to see what other shapes you can make.

What is it?

	quadrilateral	parallelogram	rhombus	rectangle	square	kite	arrowhead	trapezium
has 4 sides	✓	✓	✓	✓	✓	✓	✓	✓
all sides same length					✓			
opposite sides same length			✓					
adjacent sides same length						✓		
both pairs of opposite sides parallel				✓				
a pair of opposite sides parallel				✓				
at least 1 right angle								

1. Copy and complete the table. Only put a tick if it is true for all shapes of that type.

Now answer these questions.

2. Are all rectangles parallelograms?

3. Are all rhombuses parallelograms?

4. Are all rhombuses squares?

5. Are all squares rectangles?

6. Are all trapeziums parallelograms?

7. Are all arrowheads quadrilaterals?

8. Are all squares rhombuses?

9. Are all kites parallelograms?

10. Are all rectangles squares?

More rotating shapes

Remember: these shapes made from 4 squares are called tetrominoes.

This design was made by rotating one of the tetrominoes around its corner.

1. Draw the tetromino which was used.

2. Rotate other tetrominoes to make similar designs. You can use any point as the centre of rotation. Can your friends see which tetromino you used?

3. Pentominoes like this one are made from 5 squares. Make some rotation patterns using pentominoes.

Finding the centre of rotation

Sometimes the centre of rotation is outside a shape.

To find where the centre of rotation is, join up matching points with straight lines.

The centre of rotation is where the lines cross.

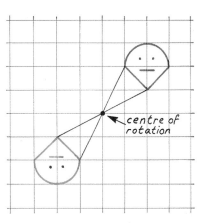

Draw these shapes on squared paper exactly as shown. Find their centres of rotation by joining matching points. You could check by tracing and then rotating the tracing paper.

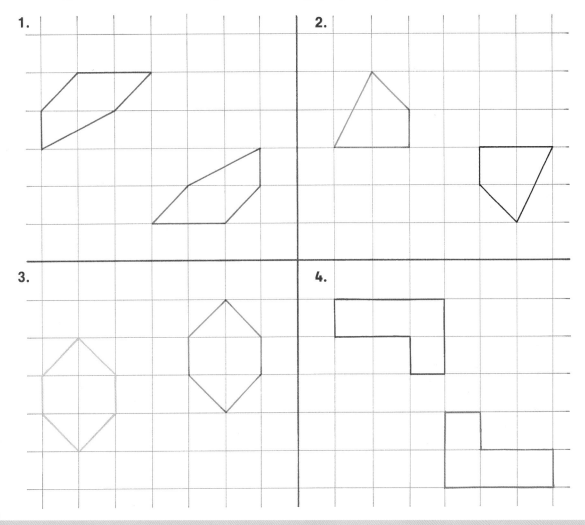

Similar and congruent figures

> **Remember:** similar figures have the same shape but may be different sizes.
> Congruent figures are the same shape and size. They are identical.

Here are some shapes:

a.   b.   c.

d.   e.   f.

1. Which shapes are congruent?

2. Which shapes are similar?

Use squared paper. Draw 2 larger shapes which are similar to these:

3.

5. Draw a triangle which is congruent to this one:

Location and transformation of shapes   Unit 7   Differentiating between similarity and congruency

Enlarging drawings

When we enlarge a shape, picture or drawing, we want each line to increase in size by the same scale factor. For example, if the scale factor is 2, each line becomes twice as long.

Melanie loved this picture of her cat so much that she had it enlarged.

3 cm

5 cm   9 cm

15 cm

Look at the dimensions (measurements) of the pictures.

1. What is the scale factor for the enlargement?

Enlarge this drawing.

2. With a scale factor of 2.

3. With a scale factor of 3.

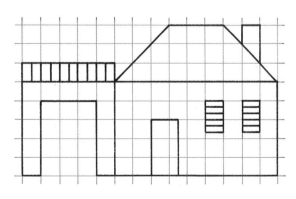

Angles in quadrilaterals ...

Since all quadrilaterals have 4 sides, they also have 4 vertices.

Draw a quadrilateral and cut it out.
Tear off the vertices and put them together.
The sum of the 4 angles should always be 360°.

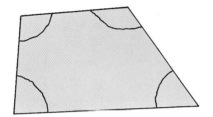

Write the measurement of the angle marked 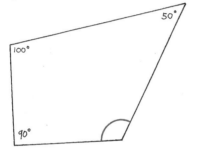 in each of these quadrilaterals.

1.

2.

3.

4.

5.

6.

... and in special quadrilaterals

In a parallelogram both pairs of opposite angles are equal.

Adjacent angles are supplementary. (They add up to 180°.)

Write the measurement of the angle marked in each of these parallelograms.

1.

45°

2.

45°

3.

100°

4.

70°

In kites and arrowheads only one pair of opposite angles is equal.
Write the measurement of the angle marked in these:

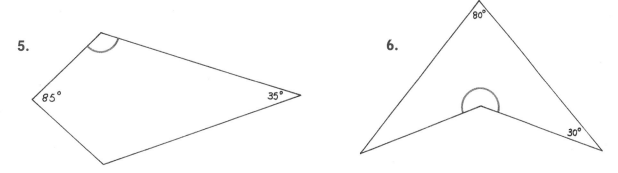

5.

85°   35°

6.

80°

30°

Angles inside polygons ...

All the possible diagonals have been drawn from one of the vertices of this pentagon.

There are only 2.
The 2 diagonals divide the pentagon into 3 triangles.

1. Compare the sum of the angles inside the pentagon with the sum of the angles in all 3 triangles.

2. Draw your own pentagon. (It does not need to be regular.) Draw the 2 diagonals from one of its vertices to make 3 triangles.

Remember: the sum of the angles inside any triangle is 180°.

3. What is the sum of the angles inside any pentagon?

4. Now divide other shapes into triangles.
   Copy and complete the chart.

shape	number of sides	number of diagonals drawn	number of triangles	sum of angles
pentagon	5	2	3	540°
hexagon	6			
octagon	8			
decagon	10			

... and outside

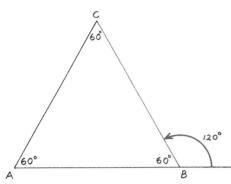

If you were walking from A to B along this triangle and you wanted to turn at B and walk up the side, you would need to turn anti-clockwise through an angle of 120°.

The exterior angle of an equilateral triangle is always 120°. (Exterior means outside.)

1. Write clear instructions for a friend to walk around an equilateral triangle with sides 10 m long. They start at a vertex and are facing along one side.

Now work out the exterior angles of:

2. a square

3. a regular pentagon

4. a regular hexagon

5. Sketch this parallelogram and write in its exterior angles.

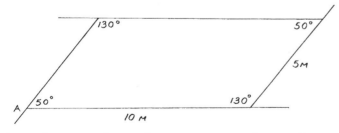

6. Write clear instructions for someone to walk around it, starting from A.

Experiment with computer turtle graphics to draw regular shapes.

Careful triangles ...

You can draw an equilateral triangle very accurately using just a pair of compasses and a ruler.

1. Draw a line   _____

    A

    Put your compass point on A and set it so that the distance between the compass point and the pencil lead is just less than the length of the line.

    Draw an arc that crosses the line.
    Call the point where it crosses B.

    Keeping your compasses set at the same distance, draw a second arc roughly where you think the top of the triangle will be.

    Now put your compass point on B and draw a third arc to cross the top one. Call this point C.

    Join A and C and B and C to make an equilateral triangle. Measure the sides of your triangle.

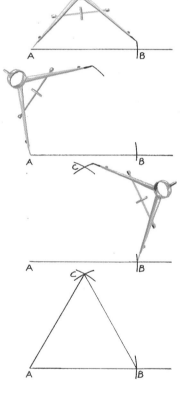

Now draw equilateral triangles with sides.

2. 5 cm   3. 8 cm

... and careful angles

You can draw an angle of 60° carefully by drawing just
2 sides of an equilateral triangle.

To draw an angle of 30° you can bisect, (split into 2 halves),
your 60° angle like this:

1. Put the compass point at A and
    mark an arc on each arm of your
    60° angle like this.
    Call these points B and C.

    Now put the compass point on B and
    mark an arc roughly halfway
    between the arms.

    Keeping your compasses set at the
    same distance, put the compass
    point on C and mark an arc across
    your halfway arc.
    Call the point where they cross D.

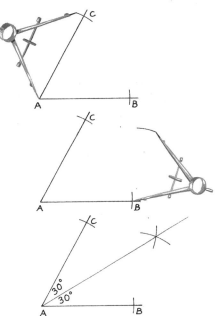

    The line joining A to D bisects the 60° angle.

Use your knowledge of drawing angles of 60° and 30° and bisecting
them to draw angles of:

2. 120°
3. 90°
4. 45°

Check with a protractor.

Choosing ways to show data

> Remember: there are many ways of showing data –
> frequency diagrams, bar charts, scatter diagrams,
> line graphs and pie charts.

Peter's progress

Peter's parents recorded his height when he was born,
and then every 6 months until he was 5 years old.

Age (years)	Birth	0.5	1	1.5	2	2.5	3	3.5	4	4.5	5
Height (cm)	50	60	72	78	82	88	90	95	100	101	105

Here is one way of showing the data:

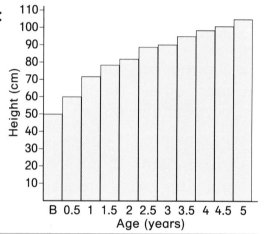

1. Make a bar-line graph to show the same data.
2. Make a line graph to show the data.
3. Which of the three graphs do you think gives the best picture of Peter's progress? Why?

A load of rubbish

In a survey of what people put in their dustbins, it was found that 36% was paper, 30% was food, 12% glass, 10% vegetation, 9% cans, and 3% other things.

4. Choose 2 good ways to show this data.
5. Which way do you think is better? Why?

What sort of diagram or graph would you use to show:

6. How you spend your day?
7. That people's shoe size is related to their height? Say why.

Rock group graphs

In the 1960s the Beatles were one of the first British rock groups to break into the American charts.

This database shows their record of success there.

Beatles' Recordings in the Top 100 (U.S.A.)									
Year	Best position	Weeks in best position	Recording	Recording label	Year	Best position	Weeks in best position	Recording	Recording label
64	1	15	I Want To Hold Your Hand	Capitol	65	68	5	Four By The Beatles	Capitol
64	14	11	I Saw Her Standing There	Capitol	65	1	10	Eight Days A Week	Capitol
64	1	15	She Loves You	Swan	65	39	6	I Don't Want to Spoil The Party	Capitol
64	3	13	Please Please Me	Vee Jay	65	1	11	Ticket To Ride	Capitol
64	41	6	From Me To You	Vee Jay	65	46	4	Yes It Is	Capitol
64	26	6	My Bonnie	MGM	65	1	13	Help	Capitol
64	2	11	Twist And Shout	Tollie	65	1	11	Yesterday	Capitol
64	74	1	There's a Place	Tollie	65	47	7	Act Naturally	Capitol
64	68	4	Roll Over Beethoven	Capitol	65	1	12	We Can Work It Out	Capitol
64	45	6	All My Loving	Capitol	65	5	10	Day Tripper	Capitol
64	1	10	Can't Buy Me Love	Capitol	66	3	9	Nowhere Man	Capitol
64	48	4	You Can't Do That	Capitol	66	81	2	What Goes On	Capitol
64	2	11	Do You Want To Know a Secret	Vee Jay	66	1	10	Paperback Writer	Capitol
64	35	7	Thank You Girl	Vee Jay	66	23	7	Rain	Capitol
64	1	14	Love Me Do	Tollie	66	2	9	Yellow Submarine	Capitol
64	10	8	P.S. I Love You	Tollie	66	11	8	Eleanor Rigby	Capitol
64	88	1	Why	MGM	67	1	10	Penny Lane	Capitol
64	92	3	Four By The Beatles	Capitol	67	8	9	Strawberry Fields Forever	Capitol
64	97	1	Sie Liebt Dich	Swan	67	1	11	All You Need Is Love	Capitol
64	1	13	A Hard Day's Night	Capitol	67	34	5	Baby You're A Rich Man	Capitol
64	53	4	I Should Have Known Better	Capitol	67	1	11	Hello Goodbye	Capitol
64	19	9	Ain't She Sweet	Atco	67	56	4	I Am The Walrus	Capitol
64	12	9	And I Love Her	Capitol	68	4	11	Lady Madonna	Capitol
64	53	9	If I Fell	Capitol	68	96	1	The Inner Light	Capitol
64	25	7	I'll Cry Instead	Capitol	68	1	19	Hey Jude	Apple
64	95	1	I'm Happy Just to Dance With You	Capitol	68	12	11	Revolution	Apple
64	17	8	Matchbox	Capitol	69	1	12	Get Back	Apple
64	25	7	Slow Down	Capitol	69	35	4	Don't Let Me Down	Apple
64	1	11	I Feel Fine	Capitol	69	8	9	The Ballad of John and Yoko	Apple
64	4	9	She's A Woman	Capitol	69	1	16	Come Together/Something	Apple

Describe the different ways that the following information could be shown. Make small drawings to help show what you mean.

If you think one way is better than the others, say so, and why.

1. The number of recordings they made with each label.

2. The length of time each record stayed in its best position.

3. How many records they had in each of the top ten positions.

4. Which years were their most successful?

5. Choose one of the graphs to draw.

Favourite meals – healthy meals?

Are favourite meals also healthy meals?

1. Use reference books to find out about different types of food, such as proteins, carbohydrates and fats.

    Find out what foods are needed for a healthy balanced diet. Write about what you find out.

    Here is some information to start you off.

Proteins	Fats	Carbohydrates	Vitamins
meat, fish, soya products GOOD FOR: body-building, growth and repair; must be part of a balanced diet HAZARDS: meat often contains fat.	dairy products, oily foods, meats GOOD FOR: storing energy, insulating the skin HAZARDS: can cause weight problems; excess of some types of fat can cause heart problems.	potatoes, bread, rice, pasta, sugary foods GOOD FOR: providing energy quickly HAZARDS: can contribute to weight problems.	salads, lightly cooked vegetables, fruit. GOOD FOR: general fitness, body repair, fighting disease. The fibre in foods such as salads is good for the digestion and blood circulation.

2. Conduct a survey of children in your class to find out their favourite meals.

    Before you start, decide what questions you are going to ask and how you are going to record the answers.

3. Sort the information you collect, and show it as a frequency diagram or a pie chart (or in some other way).

4. Write about your findings:

    What is the favourite meal? What types of food does it contain? Is it healthy and balanced?

    Are any other of the meals healthy and balanced?

5. Make a frequency table to show how many meals contained proteins, carbohydrates, fat etc.
    Draw a graph, chart of diagram. Write about your findings.

What's in your snack?

When you eat a packet snack, such as crisps or cheese puffs, what are you actually eating?

Conduct a survey of packet snack ingredients to find out.

1. Start by collecting as many different empty snack packets and bags as you can.

   Ask friends to help you.

   If you look on the back of the packets you will see the ingredients listed.

   Here are some to get you started:

   Maize meal, Vegetable oil, Starch, Chilli flavour, Acidity regulator E262, Flavour enhancer E621, Malic acid, Tartaric acid, Flavourings, Sugar, Salt, Colours E110 - E160b

   Maize meal, Vegetable oil, Starch, prawn cocktail flavour, Acidity regulator E262, Flavour enhancer E621, Citric acid, Flavourings, Artificial sweetener, Sugar, Salt, Colours E110 - E160b

   Dried potato, Vegetable oil, Potato starch, Cheese and onion flavour, Citric acid, Flavourings, Emulsifier E471, Flavour enhancers E621 - E625

2. Find out what the most common ingredients are.

   You will need to decide how you will do this.

   (You could use a tally chart or a frequency table.)

3. What are the most common additives?

   Use reference books to find out what the purpose of each additive is.

4. Make a small display or booklet about your findings.

   Remember, graphs and charts are a good way of showing information to other people.

   Ask your teacher if you could talk to the class or school about your survey.

Colour chart lucky dip

Use this colour chart with the activities on page 125.

Colour chart predictions

Look at the colour chart on page 124.
Six colours are used: red, yellow, black, green, white and blue.

To use the chart, close your eyes,
whirl your forefinger around above the chart,
then place it on the chart. (Keep your eyes closed!)
You will need to do this about 50 times.

Before you start:

1. Without counting, write down the colour you think will be touched most often. Write down the colour you think will be the next most frequent one, and the next and the next, and so on.

   There are 32 rectangles in the chart.

   There is just one white one, so the probability of a white rectangle being touched is $\frac{1}{32}$.

2. Work out the probability of each of the other colours being touched.

   List the colours in order of probability, from most probable to least probable. Does this agree with what you thought in question 1.?

3. Now use the chart 50 times. Keep a tally of your results.

4. List the colours in order of frequency from most frequent to least frequent. Do your results agree with:
   what you thought in question 1.?
   your probabilities in question 2.?

Glossary

arrowhead   A quadrilateral with two pairs of adjacent sides equal and a reflex angle.

axes   The lines, usually perpendicular, which form the reference points in a co-ordinate system.

clinometer   An instrument used to measure vertical angles.

congruent   The same shape and size.

co-ordinates   Ordered pairs used to show position on a grid, map or graph.

correlation   A relationship between two sets of data.

denominator   The bottom part of a fraction numeral, for example, the 3 in $\frac{2}{3}$.

discount   The amount by which a price is reduced. It is often written as a percentage.

factor   A factor of a number is any number that will divide into it exactly.

formula   A function expressing the relationship between two or more measures, for example, AREA = LENGTH x BREADTH.

function   A combination of operations and numbers describing something done to a number. For example, + 7 or x 4 − 4.

isosceles trapezium   A trapezium with the non-parallel sides of equal length.

isosceles triangle   A triangle with two sides of equal length and different from the third.

kite   A quadrilateral with two pairs of adjacent sides equal.

mean   A type of average. The mean of a set of data is found by adding the data and dividing the result by the number of data.

median   The middle element of an ordered set of data.

mode   The value which appears most often in a set of data. The mode of 6, 5, 6, 2, 6, is 6.

multiple   A multiple of a number is any number into which it will divide exactly.

numerator   The top part of a fraction numeral, for example, the 2 in $\frac{2}{3}$.

ordered pair   Two numbers whose order of writing is significant, for example, the x and y co-ordinates on a graph.

parallelogram   Any quadrilateral in which both pairs of opposite sides are parallel.

plane of symmetry   An imaginary slice through a solid shape dividing it into two symmetrical halves.

power   A number expressed as the result of squaring, cubing etc. For example, 16 is the second power of 4, (16 = 4 x 4), 1000 is the third power of 10, (1000 = 10 x 10 x 10).

prime factor   A prime number that is a factor of another number.

ratio   A way of comparing the size of one number or measure with another. It is found by dividing one of the numbers into the other.

recurring decimal   A fraction that cannot be expressed exactly as a decimal, but which contains a repeating string of digits. For example, $\frac{1}{11}$ = 0.090909...

reflex angle   An angle greater than two right angles and less than four right angles.

scale factor   The amount by which something is increased or reduced. A scale factor of 2 doubles the size.

scalene triangle   A triangle with all three sides of different lengths.

significant digits   Those digits that are meaningful when expressing a measure. 345 mm and 0.345 m are each expressed to three significant figures.

similar   Exactly the same shape but may be a different size.

terminating decimal   A fraction that can be expressed accurately as a decimal, for example, $\frac{3}{4} = 0.75$.

trapezium   A quadrilateral with one pair of opposite sides parallel.